THE DAILY SERVICE

REVISED EDITION

THE DAILY SERVICE

PRAYERS AND HYMNS
FOR SCHOOLS

(REVISED EDITION)

(WORDS)

Editors

PRAYERS

G. W. BRIGGS

HYMNS

PERCY DEARMER

RALPH VAUGHAN WILLIAMS

MARTIN SHAW

G. W. BRIGGS

LONDON

OXFORD UNIVERSITY PRESS

NEW YORK   TORONTO

Oxford University Press, Ely House, London W. 1

GLASGOW NEW YORK TORONTO MELBOURNE WELLINGTON
CAPE TOWN IBADAN NAIROBI DAR ES SALAAM LUSAKA ADDIS ABABA
DELHI BOMBAY CALCUTTA MADRAS KARACHI LAHORE DACCA
KUALA LUMPUR SINGAPORE HONG KONG TOKYO

The Daily Service:
first published 1936
Revised edition 1947
Revised edition (words) 1953
Thirteenth impression 1975

PRINTED IN GREAT BRITAIN

PREFACE

(1947)

THE *Daily Service* was first published in 1936, and is very widely used in its original form. But some Education Authorities (Surrey, Manchester, Gloucestershire, Worcestershire, Somerset, and Oldham) have prepared their own editions, with their own Supplement, and sometimes with matter of local interest: which is a new and welcome feature. The present edition is that adopted by the London County Council, prepared in consultation with a committee of their teachers and Inspectors.

It is obvious that the forms of prayer are optional. Moreover, the Head Teacher is free to combine them or vary them. Individual initiative is always desirable. But there is a real advantage in having the services arranged in a convenient form; and it is important in worship, as in teaching, to preserve a true balance.

Variations may be found in the Supplementary Prayers: more will be found, arranged for easy reference, in *Daily Prayer* (O.U.P.). Suitable lections, to fit the services, can be found in *The Daily Reading* (O.U.P.). References to these are given in the full-music edition: and also suggestions of suitable hymns. It seemed better to make each Service short and distinctive, and to leave room for amplification, where desired.

The responses are in italics. Musical settings for the parts marked *, as well as for the Psalms, Canticles, and Hymns, will be found in the melody and full-music editions.

Contributions have been borrowed from many

and varied sources, ancient and modern alike: for there is real unity of Christendom in its prayers, as in its great hymns.

Special acknowledgement is due to the following for copyright material: Miss A. M. Ammon (page 59); and *Book of Worship for Youth*, published by the Congregationalist and Baptist Churches (page 56); the Rt. Revd. Colin Dunlop, Dean of Lincoln (page 51); King's College, Cambridge (page 33); Messrs. A. R. Mowbray & Co., Ltd., publishers of *Memorials upon Several Occasions*, quoted as 'Memorials' (pages 49, 50); the Prayer Book Copyright Committee of the Central Board of Finance of the Church of England, from the *Prayer Book as proposed in 1928* (page 21); Messrs. Stainer & Bell, Ltd. (page 2); the late Archbishop William Temple (page 25).

The new prayers and forms in general (in the prayers section) are the copyright of Canon G. W. Briggs and the Oxford University Press. Copyright matter in the other portions of the book is acknowledged at the beginning of such portions, or underneath the items concerned.

If, through obscurity of ownership or through inadvertence, any rights still surviving have not been acknowledged, it is hoped that the owners will overlook the omission.

CONTENTS

THE LORD'S PRAYER

OUR FATHER, which art in heaven,
  Hallowed be Thy Name,
  Thy kingdom come,
  Thy will be done,
    In earth as it is in heaven.
Give us this day our daily bread.
And forgive us our trespasses,
  As we forgive them that trespass
    against us.
And lead us not into temptation;
  But deliver us from evil.
For Thine is the kingdom, the power,
    and the glory
For ever and ever. Amen.

AN ORDER OF MORNING PRAYER

(The Lord's Prayer said or sung may be added to any service. The responses are printed in italics; asterisks denote musical settings in the Melody and Full Music editions.)

I

THE SOVEREIGNTY OF GOD

THE Lord is King for ever and ever:
He sitteth upon the throne; and His judgments are over all the earth.

Thy mercy, O Lord, reacheth unto the heavens:
And Thy faithfulness unto the clouds.

Thy righteousness standeth like the strong mountains:
Thy judgments are like the great deep.

Who can measure the loving-kindness of God?
As His majesty is, so is His mercy.

THINE, O Lord, is the greatness
And the power and the glory
And the victory and the majesty;
For all that is in the heaven
And in the earth is Thine;
Thine is the kingdom,
And Thou art exalted as head over all.
Thy kingdom is an everlasting kingdom:
And Thy dominion endureth throughout all ages.

NOW unto the King eternal, immortal, invisible, the only wise God, be honour and glory for ever and ever. Amen.

II

FAITH IN GOD

THE eternal God is our refuge:
And underneath are the everlasting arms.

He holdeth our soul in life:
And suffereth not our feet to slip.

Thou, Lord, in the beginning hast laid the
foundation of the earth; and the heavens are the
work of Thy hands:
*They shall perish, but Thou remainest; they
shall be changed: but Thou art the same, and Thy
years shall not fail.*

Blessed is the man whose hope is in God.
If God be for us, who can be against us?

ALMIGHTY God, whose we are and whom we
serve: Keep us ever in Thy faith and fear,
and in obedience to Thy commandments; con-
fident that, being Thine, none can pluck us out
of Thy hand: and, fearing Thee, none can make
us afraid; through Jesus Christ our Lord. *Amen.*

Or, 'O God, the Protector', p. 41.

From 'St. Patrick's Breastplate'
Ascr. to St. Patrick, 372–466. Tr. Mrs. C. F. Alexander.

★I BIND unto myself today
  The power of God to hold and lead,
His eye to watch, his might to stay,
  His ear to hearken to my need;
The wisdom of my God to teach,
  His hand to guide, his shield to ward;
The word of God to give me speech,
  His heavenly host to be my guard.

Or Psalm 46.

III

The Indwelling God

G OD is spirit:

*And they that worship Him must worship
Him in spirit and in truth.*

God is light:
And in Him is no darkness at all.

God is love:
We love Him, because He first loved us.

God is not far from every one of us:
In Him we live and move and have our being.

E TERNAL God,
Light of the minds that know Thee,
Life of the souls that love Thee, and
Strength of the wills that serve Thee,
  Grant us so to know Thee,
  That we may truly love Thee;
So to love Thee,
  That we may fully serve Thee,
Whom to serve is perfect freedom:
  Through Jesus Christ our Lord.

Amen.

(There may be a short period of silence, after which the
prayer below may be said or sung.)

*G OD be in my head,
  And in my understanding;
God be in my eyes,
  And in my looking;
God be in my mouth,
  And in my speaking;

God be in my heart,
And in my thinking;
God be at mine end,
And at my departing.

(One of the following.)

Glory be to God,
IN whom is the fountain of life and love;
In whose light we shall see light. *Amen.*

TO God,
Whom no eye hath seen,
Nor ear hath heard,
Yet who speaks to the heart
Of all that love Him:
To Him be praise and glory for ever and ever.
Amen.

IV

GOD THE CREATOR

IN the beginning God created the heaven and
the earth:
And God created man in His own image.

As a father loves his own children:
Even so the Lord God is mindful of His own.

O Lord, our Lord, how excellent is Thy name
in all the earth!
Who hast set Thy glory upon the heavens.

When I consider Thy heavens, the work of
Thy fingers:
*The moon and the stars, which Thou hast
ordained:*

What is man, that Thou art mindful of him?
And the son of man, that Thou visitest him?

Thou hast made him but little less than divine:
And crownest him with glory and honour.

Thou madest him to have dominion over the
works of Thy hands:
Thou hast put all things under his feet.

O Lord, our Lord, how excellent is Thy name
in all the earth!

(One or both of the following.)

O GOD our Father, who hast made us in Thine
own image, with a mind to understand Thy
works, a heart to love Thee, and a will to serve
Thee: Increase in us that knowledge, love,
obedience, that we may grow daily in Thy likeness; through Jesus Christ our Lord. *Amen.*

ALMIGHTY and everlasting God, who hast
put Thine own eternity in our hearts, and
desires which the world cannot satisfy: Lift our
eyes, we pray Thee, above the narrow horizons
of this present world, that we may behold the
things eternal in the heavens, wherein is laid
up for us an inheritance that fadeth not away:
through Jesus Christ our Lord. *Amen.*

'*Our Father.*'

*IN God, who made us, God who keeps us,
Whose love will never fail us,
In Him will we trust for ever.

JESUS CHRIST OUR LORD

V

GOD so loved us, that He gave us His Son.
    *And God with Him shall freely give us all
things.*

For the childhood of Jesus in a lowly home:
For the grace and obedience of His boyhood:
For His manhood at a carpenter's bench:
    We thank Thee, O God.

For His readiness to hear His Father's call:
For His words of comfort and truth:
For His deeds of mercy and love:
    We thank Thee, O God.

For His steadfast courage and endurance:
For His death on the cross that we might live:
For His resurrection that we might rise with
    Him:
    We thank Thee, O God.

For His ascension on high: for His presence in
    our midst:
For the gift of the Holy Spirit, to guide us:
For the life that now is, and the life that is to
    come:
    Glory be to Thee, O God.

*NOW are we the sons of God, and it doth not
    yet appear what we shall be: But we know
that we shall be like Him: for we shall see Him
as He is.

VI

Our Lord Jesus Christ said:

I AM among you as he that serveth. Whosoever of you will be the chiefest, shall be servant of all.

Let us pray.

From the service of ourselves,

O Lord, set us free.

(Any of the following.)

JESUS, Friend of the friendless,
Helper of the poor,
Healer of the sick,
Whose life was spent in doing good,
Let us follow in Thy footsteps.

Make us strong to do right,
Gentle with the weak,
And kind to all who are in sorrow:
That we may be like Thee,
Our Lord and Master. Amen.

LET this mind be in *us*, which was also in Christ Jesus: who, being in the form of God, took upon him the form of a servant, and was made in the likeness of men: and being found in fashion as a man, He humbled Himself, and became obedient unto death, even the death of the cross:

Wherefore God also hath highly exalted Him,
and given Him a Name which is above every
name.

The Majesty of lowliness

O LORD Jesus Christ, in all the fulness of Thy power most gentle, in Thine exceeding greatness most humble: Bestow Thy mind and spirit upon us, who have nothing whereof to boast; that clothed in true humility, we may be exalted to true greatness. Grant this, O Lord, who livest and reignest with the Father and the Spirit, one God for evermore. *Amen.*

Adapted from the Primer of 1559, after Ludovicus Vives.

Or the prayer of Charles Kingsley, p. 44.

★ ALMIGHTY God, whose service is perfect freedom; grant us so to follow the example of thy Son Jesus Christ, that we may find our joy in service, all the days of our life. *Amen.*

VII

Jesus said:

I F any man will come after me, let him deny himself, and take up his cross, and follow me.

Let us pray.

O LORD Jesus Christ, Captain of our salvation, under whose banner we are enlisted, make us good soldiers of Thine, ready to endure hardness in Thy service: for Thy Name's sake. *Amen.*

From love of ease: from laziness and greed: from selfish refusal to serve:
> *Lord Christ, deliver us.*

From lying speech: from cowardly silence:
from the faint heart which fears the scorn of men:
from the faint heart which shrinks from suffering
pain:

Lord Christ, deliver us.

O Lord, endue us with Thy Spirit, that
we may have courage to tread the path of duty,
wherever Thou dost lead:

We beseech Thee to hear us, O Lord.

That we may have the faith which endures, as
seeing Him who is invisible:

We beseech Thee to hear us, O Lord.

That we may count it all joy to bear our cross,
as sharers of Thy Cross:

We beseech Thee to hear us, O Lord.

TEACH us, good Lord, to serve Thee as Thou
deservest; to give, and not to count the cost;
to fight, and not to heed the wounds; to toil, and
not to seek for rest; to labour, and to ask for no
reward, save that of knowing that we do Thy
will. *Amen.*   St. Ignatius Loyola, c. 1495–1556.

'Our Father.'

THE WAY OF LIFE

VIII

WHAT doth the Lord require of thee, but to
do justly, and to love mercy, and to walk
humbly with thy God?

*Lord, have mercy upon us, and write Thy law
in our hearts, we beseech Thee.*

Which is the first and great commandment?

> *Thou shalt love the Lord God with all thy heart, and with all thy soul, and with all thy mind.*
>
> *This is the first and great commandment.*
> *And the second is like unto it, Thou shalt love thy neighbour as thyself.*

Let us pray.

O GOD, who hast prepared for them that love Thee such good things as pass man's understanding: Pour into our hearts such love toward Thee, that we, loving Thee above all things, may obtain Thy promises, which exceed all that we can desire; through Jesus Christ our Lord.

> *Amen.*
> *5th century.*

*GOD be merciful unto us, and bless us; and give us grace to know His will, and strength to do it: for Jesus Christ's sake. *Amen.*

IX

BLESSED are the meek:
> *For they shall inherit the earth.*

Blessed are they which do hunger and thirst after righteousness:
> *For they shall be filled.*

Blessed are the merciful:
> *For they shall obtain mercy.*

Blessed are the pure in heart:
> *For they shall see God.*

Blessed are the peacemakers:
> *For they shall be called the children of God.*

Let us pray.

*L*ORD, *make us gentle and unselfish.*
    Help us to strive manfully for that which is
    right.
Make us merciful to all that are broken or bowed
    down.
Create in us a clean heart.
Teach us the way of peace: and let us be of them
    that make peace.

        For Jesus Christ's sake. Amen.

**D*AY by day,
        Dear Lord, of Thee three things I pray:
    To see Thee more clearly,
    Love Thee more dearly,
    Follow Thee more nearly,
Day by day.

            St. Richard of Chichester, c. 1197–1253.

X

THE GIVER OF LIFE

*A*S many as are led by the Spirit of God, they
    are the sons of God.
    And hereby we know that He abideth in us, by
    the Spirit which He hath given us.

Let us pray.

O GOD, forasmuch as without Thee we are not
    able to please Thee; Mercifully grant, that
Thy Holy Spirit may in all things direct and rule
our hearts; through Jesus Christ our Lord. *Amen.*

                5th century.

(One or both of the two following sections.)

Give us the Spirit of truth:
> *That Christ may be revealed to us; and that we may understand the deep things of God.*

Give us the Spirit of liberty:
> *That we may stand fast in the liberty wherewith Christ hath made us free.*

Give us the Spirit of unity:
> *That all who are members of the one Body may live together as members one with another.*

Give us the Spirit of power:
> *That we may be faithful witnesses to Him who has called us to His service.*

Come, Holy Ghost, our souls inspire,
> *And lighten with celestial fire.*

Come as the Breath of God:
> *And give us life.*

Come as the Tongue of Fire:
> *And cleanse and quicken us.*

Come as the Living Water:
> *And refresh us.*

Come as the rushing mighty Wind:
> *Come as the Dove, and give us peace.*

Come, Lord, in all Thy fulness:
> *And fill us with all the fulness of God.*

---

*O GOD, grant me this day the blessing and help of Thy Holy Spirit: through Jesus Christ our Lord. *Amen.*

THE CHURCH: THE FAMILY OF GOD

XI

*LIFT up your hearts:
We lift them up unto the Lord.

Let us give thanks unto our Lord God:
It is meet and right so to do.

*IT is very meet, right, and our bounden duty, that we should at all times, and in all places, give thanks unto Thee, O Lord, Holy Father, Almighty, Everlasting God.

*THEREFORE with Angels and Archangels, and with all the company of heaven, we laud and magnify Thy glorious Name; evermore praising Thee, and saying, Holy, holy, holy, Lord God of hosts, heaven and earth are full of Thy glory. Glory be to Thee, O Lord most high. *Amen.*

*FOR the Church on earth and the Church in heaven:

We praise Thee, O God.

For the multitude which no man can number, of all nations and tongues, standing before the throne:

We praise Thee, O God.

For prophets and leaders and heroes in days of old:

We praise Thee, O God.

For all who are seeking, in this our day, to do Thy will:

We praise Thee, O God.

For our fellowship with one another: for our opportunities of brave adventure in the name of Christ:

We thank Thee, O God.

*ETERNAL Father, who hast called us, Whose hand upholds us, Whose love unites us, Unto Thee be glory in the Church by Christ Jesus, throughout all ages, world without end. *Amen.*

XII

WHEREFORE, seeing we are compassed about with so great a cloud of witnesses, let us run with endurance the race that is set before us:

Looking unto Jesus, the Captain of our faith.

Let us praise God for all His faithful servants, of every age and land and nation.

For all who have given themselves, without thought of reward, for the service of God's kingdom:

Glory be to God.

For all who have braved the perils of the deep, the perils of the desert: the perils of untrodden paths, and of unknown peoples:

Glory be to God.

For all who have freed the slave from them that made merchandise of him:

Glory be to God.

For all who by the sacrifice of themselves have tamed savage hearts, and made the wilderness a garden of the Lord:

Glory be to Thee, O God.

For all faithful stewards of the Word: for all just
rulers and administrators:
> *Thanks be to God.*

For all who have laboured to heal the sick, and
to dispel the darkness and cruelty of ignorance:
> *Thanks be to God.*

For all who have been great in God's service,
whose praise is in all the world: and for the
multitude of humble men and women, who
have been content to serve unknown:
> *Thanks be to Thee, O God.*

For all who have died in faith, not having received
the promises, but having seen them afar off,
and have left to us their heritage:
> *Glory be to Thee, O Lord most high.*

Great and marvellous are Thy works, Lord God
Almighty; just and true are Thy ways, Thou
King of saints.[1]

'*Our Father.*'

(Special mention may be made at the appropriate place of
local schools, hospitals, and benefactors.)

XIII

NATURE: THE HANDIWORK OF GOD

O LORD, open Thou our lips:
And our mouth shall shew forth Thy praise.

The heavens declare Thy glory:
The sun and moon and stars obey Thy will.

---

[1] Rev. xv. 3. R.V. King of the ages.

The earth is full of Thy riches:
So is the great and wide sea also.

The eyes of all wait upon Thee, O Lord:
And Thou givest them their meat in due season.

Thou openest Thy hand:
And fillest all things living with plenteousness.

Let us pray.

FATHER, we thank Thee for all Thy gifts:
For the life-giving sun, and the life-giving
rain:
For the woods and the fields,
For the flowers and the birds,
For the rivers and the sea,
For the hills and the valleys, and
For the glory of the open sky:
For eyes to see, and health to enjoy:
Everything around us rejoices:
Make us also to rejoice, and give us thankful
hearts. *Amen.*

ALMIGHTY God, whose works are great beyond our understanding, and Thou greater
than all Thy works: Mercifully hear us, as we
endeavour to praise Thee, whom no man is able
worthily to praise; for Thy loving kindness' sake.
Amen.

O all ye works of the Lord, bless ye the Lord:
Praise Him, and magnify Him for ever.

O ye children of men, bless ye the Lord:
Praise Him, and magnify Him for ever.

*PRAISE the Lord, O my soul: and all that is
within me, praise His holy name.

XIV

Prayer

Lord, teach us to pray.

OUR Father, which art in heaven,
　Hallowed be Thy Name,
　Thy kingdom come,
　Thy will be done,
　　In earth as it is in heaven.
Give us this day our daily bread.
And forgive us our trespasses,
　As we forgive them that trespass against us.
And lead us not into temptation;
　But deliver us from evil. Amen.

FOR the faith which overcometh the world:
　For the joy of self-sacrifice, and the strength
of self-surrender:
　　We pray Thee, heavenly Father.

For the love which never faileth:
For the peace which passeth all understanding:
　　We pray Thee, heavenly Father.

For all who need our love and prayers: for all who
are sick: for all who are in sorrow:
　　Heavenly Father, hear our prayer.

(There may be a brief period of silence, and of special
remembrance.)

For all whose lives and homes are less happy than
our own:
　　Father, hear our prayer.

For all who have hurt us, by word or deed: for all
   whom we have hurt: that we may forgive, as
   we ask to be forgiven:

     Father, hear our prayer.

For light to know Thy will:
For courage to obey Thy will:
For a perfect heart to love Thy will:

     *Our Father, hear us, as we lift up our hearts
     to Thee.*

O GOD, who art nigh to all them
   That call upon Thee in truth:
   Who art Thyself the Truth,
   Whom to know is perfect knowledge:
Instruct us with Thy divine wisdom,
   And teach us Thy law;
That we may know the truth and walk in it;
Through Him in whom the truth was made
     manifest,
Even Jesus Christ, Thy Son, our Lord. *Amen.*
     From Christian Prayers, 1578 *(after St. Augustine)*

*ENRICH, Lord, heart, mouth, hands in me,
   With faith, with hope, with charity:
That I may run, rise, rest with Thee.
     George Herbert, 1593–1632

XV

PENITENCE

IF we say that we have no sin, we deceive ourselves, and the truth is not in us.

   *If we confess our sins, He is faithful and just to
forgive us our sins, and to cleanse us from all un-
righteousness.*

Let us ask God for forgiveness.

*A*LMIGHTY *God, have mercy upon us, forgive us all our sins, and deliver us from all evil, confirm and strengthen us in all goodness, and bring us to life everlasting: through Jesus Christ our Lord. Amen.*

From all evil-doing and evil-speaking: from all evil thoughts that poison the mind:
> *Good Lord, deliver us.*

From all dishonesty in word or deed: from indifference to the needs of others: from selfish use of the gifts which Thou hast entrusted to us:
> *Good Lord, deliver us.*

From all mean ambitions; from all faintheartedness in serving Thee; from all unwillingness to take up our cross:
> *Good Lord, deliver us.*

(Here may be a short period of silence.)

O Saviour of the world, who by Thy cross and precious blood hast redeemed us:
> *Save us, and help us, we humbly beseech Thee, O Lord.*

(Here again there may be silence, after which shall be said:)

He was wounded for our transgressions, He was bruised for our iniquities: and with His stripes we are healed.
> *Thanks be to God for His unspeakable gift.*

*UNTO Him that loved us, and washed us from our sins in His own blood, and hath made us kings and priests unto God and His Father, Unto Him be glory, and dominion, For ever and ever. *Amen.*

XVI

THE SPREAD OF THE KINGDOM

Let us pray that God's Kingdom may be spread over all the world.

>*Thy kingdom come, O God.*

For all who know and love Thee:
For all who once loved Thee, but have forgotten Thee:

>*Lord, hear our prayer.*

For all who have never known Thee:
For them that sit in darkness, without hope in God:

>*Lord, hear our prayer.*

For all who are carrying the good news, both at home and in other lands:

>*Lord, teach us to pray.*

For ourselves: that we may take our share in passing on the glad tidings which we have heard:

>*Lord, teach us to pray.*

BLESS, O Lord, all who bear witness in Thy name, by teaching, by healing, by leadership, in the far outposts of the world; and set our hearts on fire to serve Thee, and to spread Thy Kingdom; for Jesus Christ's sake. *Amen.*

*THE earth shall be full of the knowledge of the Lord, as the waters cover the sea.

SPECIAL OCCASIONS

XVII

QUEEN AND COUNTRY

O LORD, save the Queen;
Who putteth her trust in Thee.

Send her help from Thy holy place;
And evermore mightily defend her.

Accession Service, 1576, &c.

The Queen and all in authority under her

ALMIGHTY God, the fountain of all goodness, we humbly beseech Thee to bless our Sovereign Lady, Queen *ELIZABETH*, the Parliaments in all her dominions, and all who are set in authority under her; that they may order all things in wisdom, righteousness, and peace, to the honour of Thy holy Name, and the good of Thy Church and people; through Jesus Christ our Lord. *Amen.* *After Prayer Book, 1928.*

Ourselves

GOD of our fathers, who through many generations hast led us on our way: Give us all such an obedience to Thy will, and faithfulness in Thy service, as may declare us to be Thy people: to the glory of Thy holy Name. *Amen.*

See also The Saints of our own land, p. 49.

For this God is our God for ever and ever:
He will be our guide even unto death.

'Our Father.'

Psalm 46.

XVIII

THE COMMONWEALTH

BLESSED is the people, O Lord, that can
rejoice in Thee:
They shall walk in the light of Thy countenance.
Their delight shall be daily in Thy name:
*And in Thy righteousness shall they make their
boast.*

The Queen. [See p. 21.]

The Commonwealth

ALMIGHTY God, Father of all men, under
whose providence we are become members of
a great commonwealth of nations, and have in our
keeping the government and protection of many
peoples: Give us such a spirit of wisdom and
understanding, of justice and truth, of knowledge
and of the fear of the Lord, that all the nations
and peoples of this Commonwealth may ever
abide in one bond of fellowship and service; to
the glory of Thy Name. Through Jesus Christ
our Lord. *Amen.*

Any prayers from p. 23.

'Our Father.'

Jubilate, p. 24.

XIX

The Whole World

THE earth is the Lord's, and the fulness thereof:
The round world, and they that dwell therein.

From the rising of the sun unto the going down of the same:
His name shall be glorified.

O GOD, the Creator of the ends of the earth, with whom there is no distinction of race or habitation, but all are one in Thee: Break down, we beseech Thee, the barriers which divide us; that we may work together in one accord with each other and with Thee; through Him who is the Saviour of all, Jesus Christ Thy Son our Lord. *Amen.*

ALMIGHTY God, from whom all thoughts of truth and peace proceed: Kindle, we pray Thee, in the hearts of all men the true love of peace, and guide with Thy pure and peaceable wisdom those who take counsel for the nations of the earth; that in tranquillity Thy kingdom may go forward, till the earth is filled with the knowledge of Thy love; through Jesus Christ our Lord. *Amen.*   *Bishop Paget of Oxford (1851–1911).*

ALMIGHTY God, Maker of all things, who hast placed Thy creatures necessary for the use of man in diverse lands: Grant that all men and nations, needing one another, may be knit together in one bond of mutual service, to share

their diverse riches; through Jesus Christ our
Lord. *Amen.*   16th century *(adapted).*

'*Our Father.*'

Psalm 100 following, or Psalm 98.

Psalm C. *Jubilate Deo*

★O BE joyful in the **Lord,** | all ye | lands : serve
the Lord with gladness, ★ and **come** before
his | presence | with a | song.

2 Be ye **sure** that the | Lord · he is | God : it
is he that hath made us, and not we ourselves; ★
we are his **people** and the | sheep of | his — |
pasture.

3 O go your way into his gates with thanks-
giving, ★ and **into** his | courts with | praise : be
thankful unto **him** and | speak good | of his |
Name.

4 For the Lord is gracious, ★ his **mercy** is |
ev-er- | lasting : and his truth endureth from
gener- | ation · to | gen-er- | ation.

Glory | be · to the | Father : and to the **Son,** |
and · to the | Ho-ly | Ghost;

As it was in the beginning, is **now** and | ever |
shall be : **world** without end. | A- | — | men.

XX

FOR ALL WORKERS

THE body is not one member, but many. If
one member suffer, all the members suffer
with it.

Bear ye one another's burdens:
And also fulfil the law of Christ.

Let us pray for all who supply the needs of our common life; that we may all be faithful in sharing the common burden.

For all who labour in the fields, at home and abroad, to grow our food:

Lord, hear our prayer:

And let our cry come unto Thee.

(This to be repeated after each petition.)

FOR all who work in mine and factory, in shop and office:

For all who brave the seas to bring the produce of other lands; and for all who transport it, by road and rail and air:

For all inventors, who by their skill open out new discoveries; and for all who direct our labours for the common good:

For doctors and nurses, in their vocation of healing; for writers and preachers and teachers, and all who labour to impart true knowledge; and for all places of education and learning:

For all members of the one body, that they may serve faithfully in their several callings:

Lord, hear our prayer:

And let our cry come unto Thee.

O GOD, the King of righteousness, lead us, we pray Thee, in the ways of justice and of peace; inspire us to break down all oppression and wrong, to gain for every man his due reward, and from every man his due service; that each

may live for all, and all may care for each; in the
Name of Jesus Christ our Lord. *Amen.*

Archbishop William Temple, 1881–1944.

PRESERVE us, O Lord, from the meanness of
spirit which is content to reap and sow not; to
labour not, but to live on other men's labours; for
Thy mercy's sake. *Amen.*

REMEMBER the words of the Lord Jesus,
how He said, It is more blessed to give than
to receive.

'*Our Father.*'

Psalm 15.

XXI

THE QUEEN'S FORCES

Strive for the truth unto death:
And the Lord God shall fight for thee.

The Queen's Forces

O ALMIGHTY Lord God, the Father and
Protector of them that trust in Thee: We
commend to Thy fatherly care the Forces of the
Crown, by sea, by land, and in the air; beseeching
Thee to take into Thine own hand both them and
the cause they serve. Be Thou their strength when
they are set in the midst of so many and great
dangers. Make all bold through life or death to
put their trust in Thee, who canst save by many
or by few; through Jesus Christ our Lord. *Amen.*

Archbishop Benson, 1885 (adapted).

The Armour of God

ARM us, O Lord, with the whole armour of God, with the shield of faith,
> the sword of the Spirit,
> the helmet of salvation,
> the girdle of truth,
> the breastplate of righteousness,

that we may be able to stand in the evil day;
And let our feet be shod
> with the preparation of the gospel of peace,

that, having done all, we may stand in the same,
now and for ever. *Amen.* Ephesians vi.

GIVE peace in our time, O Lord:
> *For there is none other that fighteth for us,
> but only Thou, O God.*

'Our Father.'

(*To be said or sung.*)

May the peace of God rule in our hearts. *Amen.*

Psalm 46.

XXII

FOR THOSE AT SEA

THEY that go down to the sea in ships:
> *And occupy their business in great waters:*

These men see the works of the Lord:
> *And His wonders in the deep.*

ALMIGHTY and everlasting God, who art everywhere present: we commend to Thy fatherly care all whose way is on the sea. Help them, in whatever lies before them, to quit themselves like men. If there be any duty, may they do it with cheerfulness: if any danger, may they face it with courage: knowing that Thy hand is in all things, and all things are in Thy hand. We ask it for Thy Name's sake. *Amen.*

The Royal Navy

(From a prayer used daily in Her Majesty's ships.)

O ETERNAL Lord God, who alone spreadest out the heavens, and rulest the raging of the sea: who hast compassed the waters with bounds until day and night come to an end: Be pleased to receive into Thy Almighty and most gracious protection the persons of Thy servants, and the Fleets in which they serve. Preserve them from the dangers of the sea, and from the violence of the enemy; that they may be a safeguard unto our Sovereign Lady, Queen *ELIZABETH*, and her Dominions, and a security for such as pass on the seas upon their lawful occasions; that the inhabitants of the Commonwealth may in peace and quietness serve Thee our God; through Jesus Christ our Lord. *Amen.*

For fishermen

ALMIGHTY and all-merciful Father, who rulest in heaven and earth and sea, and in all deep places; at whose word the stormy wind ariseth, and again at Thy word the great calm: Receive into Thy protection Thy servants the fishermen, in their honest calling; that through calm or storm they may come in with safety: for the sake of Him who stilled the waves, Jesus Christ our Lord. *Amen.*

(*Adapted from the Clovelly Fishermen's Prayer.*)

'Our Father.'

XXIII

FOR ALL WHO TRAVEL BY AIR

O LORD my God, Thou art very great:
Thou art clothed with honour and majesty:

Who deckest Thyself with light as with a garment:
Who stretchest out the heavens like a curtain:

Who makest the clouds Thy chariots:
Who walkest upon the wings of the wind.

Whither shall I go then from Thy Spirit?
Or whither shall I flee from Thy presence?

If I climb up into heaven, Thou art there:
If I take the wings of the morning, and dwell in the uttermost parts of the sea:

Even there shall Thy hand lead me:
And Thy right hand shall hold me.

From Psalms 104, 139

Let us pray.

ETERNAL God, who dwellest afar in the heavens, yet abidest in the hearts of the sons of men: We beseech Thee for all who journey across the trackless spaces of the air, that they may know Thee near them, to pilot and to protect: through Jesus Christ our Lord. *Amen.*

'Our Father.'

Psalm 19.

XXIV

The School

HAPPY is the man that findeth wisdom:
And the man that getteth understanding.

For the merchandise of it is better than the merchandise of silver:
And the gain thereof than fine gold.

She is a tree of life to them that lay hold upon her:
And happy is every man that retaineth her.

The fear of the Lord, that is wisdom:
And to depart from evil is understanding.

(Any of the following.)

The School

BLESS, O Lord, we beseech Thee, this our school: take away whatsoever is unworthy, cherish and strengthen whatsoever is best in it. And grant that all who go forth hence may manfully fight Thy battles in the world, and conquer through the might of Jesus Christ our Lord. *Amen.*　　*School Prayers for Week-day Mornings.*

The Home

O GOD our Father, bless our homes, and make them Thy dwelling-place. Keep us faithful to Thee, and helpful to one another; for the sake of Him who shared an earthly home at Nazareth, Jesus Christ Thy Son our Lord. *Amen.*

The Wisdom of Life

LORD, give us wisdom,
  Early to know Thy will,
Steadfastly to do it:
  For Jesus Christ's sake. *Amen.*

True education

MAKE us wise, O Lord,
  To know what Thou wouldst have us know,
That we may do what Thou wouldst have us do,
And be what Thou wouldst have us be;
  For Jesus Christ's sake. *Amen.*

For teachableness

HEAR our prayers, O Lord Jesu, the everlasting Wisdom of the Father; who givest
unto us, in the days of our youth, aptness to
learn: Add, we pray Thee, the furtherance of Thy
grace, so to learn knowledge and the liberal
sciences that, by their help, we may attain to the
fuller knowing of Thee, whom to know is the
height of blessedness; and by the example of Thy
boyhood, may duly increase in age, wisdom, and
favour with God and man. Who livest and
reignest with the Father and the Holy Ghost,
world without end. *Amen.*

Erasmus, 1467–1536; slightly shortened.
Composed for St. Paul's School, probably
at the request of Dean Colet.

Humility

O GOD, the only Wise, whose Son, Jesus
  Christ, sat lowly in the midst of the doctors,
both hearing them and asking them questions:
Grant us that humility of heart, and willingness
to learn, without which no man can find wisdom;
through the same Jesus Christ our Lord. *Amen.*

Beginning of Term

O GOD, we pray Thee to bless our work this term. Give us a true love of learning: and grant that in everything we learn we may learn more of Thee. For Jesus Christ's sake. *Amen.*

Newcomers

LET Thy blessing, O God, be upon all who are newly entered into our family; that they may inherit, and pass on to them that follow, all that is best in our traditions; through Jesus Christ our Lord. *Amen.*

End of Term. For those leaving the School

WE commend, O Lord, unto Thy fatherly care Thy servants about to leave this school, beseeching Thee that Thy loving-kindness and mercy may follow them all the days of their life. Succour them in temptation, preserve them in danger, assist them in every good work, and keep them ever in the right way. And grant, O Father, that by Thy merciful aid we may so walk before Thee in this life, that we may all meet again in Thy eternal Kingdom; through Jesus Christ our Lord. *Amen.*   *School Prayers for Week-day Mornings.*

Commemoration

O LORD God, the Father of lights, the Maker and Builder of every house not made with hands: We give Thee thanks for all members of this school who have served Thee with fruitful labour for the increase of knowledge and wisdom, and for the nurture of faithful servants of Thy Church and Kingdom. As Thou didst enable them to add their share to Thy work, wrought out by many hands from age to age, so teach and

strengthen us, we pray Thee, to do Thy will in
the task which Thou hast apportioned us in this
our generation; and grant that with them we may
enter into Thy joy in the fulfilment of Thine
eternal counsel; through Jesus Christ our Lord.
Amen.   *Date unknown. Eton and King's College,*
                              Cambridge and other foundations.

> Glory be to God,
> The fountain of all wisdom,
> In whose light we shall see light.

Amen.

Psalm 1.

XXV

CHRISTMAS

A Bidding Prayer before a Christmas Carol Service

(*Adapted, by permission, from the service at King's College,
Cambridge.*)

BE it this Christmastide our care and delight to
prepare ourselves to hear again the message of
the Angels, and in heart and mind to go even unto
Bethlehem and see this thing which is come to
pass, and the Babe lying in a manger:

Let us read and mark in Holy Scripture the tale
of the loving purposes of God from the first days
of our disobedience unto the glorious Redemption
brought us by this Holy Child: and let us make
this place glad with our carols of praise:

But first let us pray for the needs of His whole
world; for peace and goodwill over all the earth;
for unity and brotherhood within the Church He

came to build, and especially in the dominions of our sovereign lady Queen Elizabeth; and within this city (town, village):

And because this of all things would rejoice His heart, let us at this time remember in His name the poor and the helpless, the cold, the hungry, and the oppressed; the sick and them that mourn; the lonely and the unloved; the aged and the little children; all those who know not the Lord Jesus, or who love Him not, or who by sin have grieved His heart of love:

Lastly, let us remember before God all those who rejoice with us, but upon another shore and in a greater light, that multitude which no man can number, whose hope was in the Word made flesh, and with whom, in this Lord Jesus, we for evermore are one:

These prayers and praises let us humbly offer up to the Throne of Heaven, in the words which Christ Himself hath taught us:

*O*UR Father, which art in heaven,
   Hallowed be Thy Name,
   Thy kingdom come,
   Thy will be done,
     In earth as it is in heaven.
Give us this day our daily bread.
And forgive us our trespasses,
   As we forgive them that trespass against us.
And lead us not into temptation;
   But deliver us from evil.

For Thine is the kingdom, the power, and the glory,
For ever and ever. Amen.

The Almighty God bless us with His grace: Christ give us the joys of everlasting life: and

unto the fellowship of the citizens above may the
King of Angels bring us all. *Amen.*

———

Suitable passages for reading: Isa. ix. 2. 6; Luke i. 26–33;
Luke ii. 1–7; Luke ii. 8–14; Luke ii. 15–20; Matt. ii. 1–12;
John i. 1–14. It is more effective if the reading is not
announced and simply ends with 'Thanks be to God'.
Carols come between the readings.

———

For Ash Wednesday see Service XV and Collect for Lent,
p. 56.

XXVI

EASTERTIDE

NOW is Christ risen from the dead:
 The firstfruits of them that slept.

O death, where is thy sting?
 O grave, where is thy victory?

Thanks be to God, who giveth us the victory,
 Through our Lord Jesus Christ.

See Eastertide, p. 57.

(There may be a brief period of silent remembrance, and
after it the following prayer.)

ALMIGHTY and everliving God, we bless Thy
holy Name for all Thy servants departed this
life in Thy faith and fear, especially those most
dear to us; beseeching Thee to give us grace so
to follow their good examples, that with them
we may be partakers of Thy heavenly kingdom;
through the resurrection of Jesus Christ our
Redeemer. *Amen.*   *Adapted from* 1549.

'Our Father.'

NOW the God of peace, that brought again from the dead our Lord Jesus, that great Shepherd of the sheep, through the blood of the everlasting covenant, make *us* perfect in every good work to do His will, working in *us* that which is well-pleasing in His sight, through Jesus Christ; to whom be glory for ever and ever. *Amen.*

Hebrews xiii.

XXVII

ASCENSION DAY

CHRIST sitteth on the right hand of God:
In the glory of the Father.

When He ascended on high, He led captivity captive:
And gave gifts unto men.

Who shall ascend into the hill of the Lord?
Or who shall rise up in His holy place?

Even he that hath clean hands and a pure heart:
And that hath not lift up his mind unto vanity, nor sworn to deceive his neighbour.

He shall receive the blessing from the Lord:
And righteousness from the God of his salvation.

Let us pray.

GRANT, we beseech Thee, Almighty God, that like as we do believe Thy only-begotten Son our Lord Jesus Christ to have ascended into the heavens; so we may also in heart and mind thither ascend, and with Him continually dwell, who liveth and reigneth with Thee and the Holy Ghost, one God, world without end. *Amen.*

6th century.

See also The Christian Year, p. 57, and Te Deum, Part II, p. 39.

XXVIII

Harvest

WHILE the earth remaineth, seed-time and harvest, and cold and heat, and summer and winter, and day and night, shall not cease.

See (in whole or part) Service XIII.

O GOD the Father of us all, we thank Thee for Thy gift of harvest. Bless all who sowed and all who reaped: and make us glad to share Thy gifts with all Thy children. For Jesus Christ's sake. *Amen.*

The Bread of Life

MOST bountiful Father, on whose providence we do wholly depend: Give us daily at Thy pleasure whatsoever the necessity of this life requireth; but above all feed our souls with spiritual food, with the bread of life from heaven; through Jesus Christ our Lord. *Amen.*

From Christian Prayers, 1578 (after Erasmus).

See General Thanksgiving, p. 54; also Psalm 65, p. 67.

XXIX

Adoration

Gloria in Excelsis

*Glory be to | God on | high, || and in **earth** |
peace, good | will towards | men. ||

We **praise** thee, we **bless** thee, we | worship |
thee, || we glorify thee, we give **thanks** to | thee
for | thy great | glory, ||

O Lord **God**, | heavenly | King, || **God** the |
Father | Al- | mighty. ||

O Lord, the only-begotten **Son** | Jesu |
Christ; || *O Lord God, Lamb of God,* | *Son* | *of the* |
Father, ||

That takest away the **sins** | of the | world, ||
have | *mer-* | *cy up-* | *on us.* ||

Thou that takest away the **sins** | of the |
world, || *have* | *mer-* | *cy up-* | *on us.* ||

Thou that takest away the **sins** | of the |
world, || *re-* | *ceive* | *our* | *prayer.* ||

Thou that sittest at the right **hand** of | God
the | Father, || *have* | *mer-* | *cy up-* | *on us.* ||

For **thou** | only art | holy; || thou | only | art
the | Lord; ||

Thou only, **O Christ**, with the | Holy |
Ghost, || art most **high** in the | glory of | God
the | Father. || A-men.

NOTE. *The second part may be sung antiphonally, the break
        being marked by italics.*

See also p. 54, 'Before the glorious throne', and p. 60,
        'To God, the blessed and only Potentate'.

XXX

Te Deum

Part I

*WE **praise** | thee O | God : we ac**know**ledge |
thee to | be the | Lord.

2 All the **earth** doth | worship | thee : the |
Father | ever- | lasting.

3 To thee all **An**gels | cry a-| loud : the **Heavens**
and | all the | Powers there- | in.

4 To **thee** | Cherubin and | Seraphin : con- |
tinual- | ly do | cry,

5 **Holy** | Holy | Holy : **Lord** | God of | Saba- |
oth.

6 **Heaven** and | earth are | **full** : of the |
Majesty | of thy | Glory.

7 The glorious **comp**any of the A- | postles |
praise thee : The goodly **fell**owship of the | Pro-
phets | praise — | thee :

8 The noble **army** of | Martyrs | praise thee :
The holy Church throughout all the **world** |
doth ac- | know-ledge | thee.

[*2nd part*] 9 The **Father** of an | infinite |
Majesty : Thine honourable true and only Son,*
also the | Holy | Ghost the | Comforter.

Part II

*10 Thou art the **King** of | Glory O | Christ :
Thou art the ever- | **last-ing** | Son · of the |
Father.

11 When thou tookest u**pon** thee to de- | liver |
man : Thou **didst** not ab- | hor the | Virgin's |
womb.

[*2nd part*] 12 When thou hadst over**come**
the | sharpness of | death : thou didst open the
Kingdom of | Heaven to | all be- | lievers.

13 Thou sittest at the **right** | hand of | God;
in the | glory | of the | Father.

14 **We** be- | lieve that | **thou shalt** | come to |
be our | judge.

15 We therefore **pray** thee | help thy | ser-
vants : whom thou hast re**deem**ed | with thy |
precious | blood.

16 Make them to be **num**bered | with thy |
Saints : in | glory | ev-er- | lasting.

The Third Part of the Te Deum is omitted here. It was
a later addition, consisting of versicles and responses, which
should be sung as such.

See also p. 55, 'Lord God Almighty and All-merciful',
and p. 60, 'Blessing, and honour, and glory'.

SUPPLEMENTARY PRAYERS

I–IV. God our Father

O GOD, the Protector of all that trust in Thee, without whom nothing is strong, nothing is holy: Increase and multiply upon us Thy mercy; that, Thou being our ruler and guide, we may so pass through things temporal, that we finally lose not the things eternal: Grant this, O heavenly Father, for Jesus Christ's sake our Lord. *Amen.*

6th century.

LORD of all power and might, who art the Author and Giver of all good things; Graft in our hearts the love of Thy Name, increase in us true religion, nourish us with all goodness, and of Thy great mercy keep us in the same; through Jesus Christ our Lord. *Amen.*   *5th century.*

O GOD, who art in every place, making Thy dwelling-place holy ground: Fill our hearts with awe and wonder as we pass along the common ways of life; that in them we may behold Thee, and beholding bow down before Thy presence; through Jesus Christ our Lord. *Amen.*

Eternity

O GOD, who art from everlasting to everlasting, with whom a thousand years are but as yesterday: Hallow the life which Thou hast given to us; that living with Thee in this passing world, we may live with Thee, and in Thee, to all eternity: through Jesus Christ our Lord. *Amen.*

The growth of knowledge

ALMIGHTY God, who hast given us powers which our fathers never knew, to probe Thine ancient mysteries, and to discover Thy hidden treasures: Quicken our conscience, we beseech Thee, as Thou dost enlighten our understanding; lest, having tasted the fruits of knowledge, we perish through our own pride and disobedience. We ask it for Jesus Christ's sake. *Amen.*

ALMIGHTY God, in whom we live and move, and have our being; who hast made us for Thyself, so that we can find rest only in Thee: Grant us purity of heart and strength of purpose, so that no selfish passion shall hinder us from knowing Thy will, no weakness keep us from doing it. In Thy light may we see light, and in Thy service find our freedom and our strength: through Jesus Christ our Lord. *Amen.*

After St. Augustine, 354–430.

O GOD, who art the portion of our inheritance,
    Be Thou unto us all in all,
    Our light in darkness,
    Our strength in weakness,
    Our only desire, and our sure reward;
            for Jesus Christ's sake.   *Amen.*

V–VII. OUR LORD JESUS CHRIST

O LORD Jesus Christ, who hast deigned to be made like unto men; the sharer of our sorrows, the companion of our journeys, the light of our ignorance, the remedy of our infirmity: So fill us with Thy Spirit, and endue us with Thy grace, that as Thou hast been made like unto us, we may grow more like unto Thee; for Thy mercy's sake. *Amen.*

Freely adapted from Jeremy Taylor, 1613–67.

The compassion of Christ

ALMIGHTY God, whose Son, our Lord and Saviour Jesus Christ, was moved with compassion for all who had gone astray, with indignation for all who suffered wrong: Inflame our hearts with the burning fire of Thy love, that with Him we may seek out the lost, have mercy on the fallen, and stand fast for truth and righteousness: through the same Jesus Christ our Lord. *Amen.*

The faith of Christ

O LORD Jesus Christ, who in the days of Thy flesh didst reveal by Thine own faith the sure victory of faith: Grant us by the Holy Spirit the same faith, steadfast and unconquerable, that we also may do the works of God, with whom all things are possible; to the glory of His holy Name. *Amen.*

Suffering with Christ

O SON of God, who for us men hast drained the cup of sacrifice: Enable us by Thy grace to drink of Thy cup, and to rejoice that unto us it is given, not only to believe in Thee, but also to suffer with Thee; to the glory of Thy Name. *Amen.*

ALMIGHTY and everlasting God, who, of Thy tender love towards mankind, has sent Thy Son, our Saviour Jesus Christ, to take upon Him our flesh and to suffer death upon the cross, that

all mankind should follow the example of His
great humility; Mercifully grant, that we may
both follow the example of His patience, and also
be made partakers of His resurrection; through
the same Jesus Christ our Lord. *Amen.*

5th century.

CHRIST be with me. Christ within me,
Christ before me, Christ beside me.
    Christ to win me,
Christ to comfort and restore me,
Christ beneath me, Christ above me,
Christ in quiet, Christ in danger,
Christ in hearts of all that love me,
Christ in mouth of friend and stranger.

Attributed to St. Patrick (c. 372–466).

VIII–IX. THE WAY OF LIFE

O ALMIGHTY God, who alone canst order
the unruly wills and affections of sinful men:
Grant unto Thy people, that they may love the
thing which Thou commandest, and desire that
which Thou dost promise; that so, among the
sundry and manifold changes of the world, our
hearts may surely there be fixed, where true joys
are to be found; through Jesus Christ our Lord.
Amen.   *5th century.*

TAKE from us, O heavenly Father, all pride
and vanity, all boasting and forwardness, and
give us the true courage that shows itself by
gentleness; the true wisdom that shows itself by
simplicity; and the true power that shows itself
by modesty and thought for others; through Jesus
Christ our Lord. *Amen.* *Charles Kingsley (1819–75).*

O GOD of all goodness, whose greatest gifts are Thy simplest gifts, bestowed on men of all estates:

    Give us Thy blessings,
        Love and peace, and gladness of heart,
        Health of body and mind,
        And the joy of serving Thee;
            through Jesus Christ our Lord. *Amen.*

X. The Giver of Life

The Spirit of purity

ALMIGHTY God, unto whom all hearts be open, all desires known, and from whom no secrets are hid: Cleanse the thoughts of our hearts by the inspiration of Thy holy Spirit, that we may perfectly love Thee, and worthily magnify Thy holy Name: through Christ our Lord. *Amen.*

Ancient.

The Spirit of truth

LEAD us, O Lord God, by the Spirit of truth; that, hating and abhorring all that maketh a lie, we may find in the truth our freedom; through Jesus Christ our Lord. *Amen.*

The Spirit of power

ALMIGHTY God, without whose aid we can do nothing: Endue us with Thy Spirit of power from on high, that out of weakness we may be made strong; through Jesus Christ our Lord. *Amen.*

LET Thy mighty hand, O Lord God, and outstretched arm be our defence; Thy mercy and loving kindness in Jesus Christ, Thy dear Son,

our salvation; Thy all-true word our instruction;
the grace of Thy life-giving Spirit our comfort
and consolation, unto the end and in the end.
Amen.   *Knox's Book of Common Order,* 1564.

XI–XII. THE CHURCH: THE FAMILY OF GOD

The Communion of Saints

ETERNAL Father, of whom the whole family
in heaven and earth is named: Unite us, as
we worship Thee here, with all who in far-off
places are lifting up their hands and hearts to
Thee; that Thy Church throughout the world,
with the Church in heaven, may offer up one
sacrifice of thanksgiving; to the praise of Thy
Holy Name: through Jesus Christ our Lord.

Amen.

THERE is one body and one Spirit,
  even as we are called in one hope of our calling:
    One Lord, one faith, one baptism.
    One God and Father of all,
    who is above all, and through all,
      and in us all.   St. Paul.

THE LORD'S DAY

O GOD, give Thy people grace to use aright
Thy holy day; that it may be a day of mercy
to the heavy-laden; a day of resurrection to new-
ness of life; a day to worship Thee in the fellowship of the faithful; through Jesus Christ our
Lord. *Amen.*

(NOTE.—'*The Lord's day*'—*hence its name*—*is primarily the
weekly memorial of the Resurrection: but it also inherits the
humane tradition of the ancient day of mercy. See* Deut. v.
14; *and our Lord's comment,* Matt. xii. 7.)

XIII. NATURE: THE HANDIWORK OF GOD

God's care for little things

LORD of infinite greatness, who hast ordered and adorned in equal perfection all that Thou hast made; who hast set in glorious array the eternal heavens, and yet dost paint the lily that abideth but a few days: Give us courage to attempt great things in Thy Name, and equal faithfulness to do the small; to Thy honour and glory; through Jesus Christ our Lord. *Amen.*

The countryside

O GOD, who hast made all things beautiful: Give us a love of Thy countryside, its lanes and meadows, its woods and streams, and clean open spaces; and let us keep it fresh and unspoilt for those who shall come after us; for Jesus Christ's sake. *Amen.*

BLESSED be God in all His gifts: and holy in all His works.   *Primer, 1559.*

XIV. PRAYER

GOD, who art mighty, and despisest not any: Have mercy upon us in our weakness, and in Thy strength make us strong: for Jesus Christ's sake. *Amen.*

Mercy

FATHER of all mercies, teach us to be merciful, as Thou art merciful: knowing that, with what measure we mete, it shall be measured to us again.

For Jesus Christ's sake. *Amen.*

The Tongue

SET a watch, O Lord, upon our tongue:
that we may never speak the cruel word which
is untrue;
or, being true, is not the whole truth;
or, being wholly true, is merciless;
for the love of Jesus Christ our Lord. *Amen.*

LET this day, O Lord, add some knowledge or good
deed to yesterday.   *Bishop Andrewes (c.* 1555–1626).

O LORD, never suffer us to think that we can
stand by ourselves, and not need Thee.
*John Donne (*1573–1631*), Dean of St. Paul's.*

O LORD, Thou knowest how busy I must be this
day. If I forget Thee, do not Thou forget me.
Sir Jacob Astley (before the battle of Edgehill, 1642).

O GOD, help us not to despise or oppose what we
do not understand.   *William Penn (*1644–1718).

LORD, let me not live to be useless.
*John Wesley (*1703–91*), from Bishop Stratford.*

LORD, who hast given all for us: help us to give all
for Thee.

XV. PENITENCE

'*Whatsoever a man soweth*'

O GOD, by whose unchanging law the harvest
follows the seed-time, and whatsoever is sown
is afterward reaped: Mercifully grant that we sow
not such seed, that we and they who follow after
us reap misery and shame.
For Jesus Christ's sake. *Amen.*

XVI. THE SPREAD OF THE KINGDOM

O GOD, who hast made of one blood all
nations of men for to dwell on the face of
the earth, and didst send Thy blessed Son Jesus
Christ to preach peace to them that are afar off,
and to them that are nigh: Grant that all the
peoples of the world may feel after Thee and find
Thee; and hasten, O God, the fulfilment of Thy
promise, to pour out Thy Spirit upon all flesh;
through Jesus Christ our Lord. *Amen.*

Bishop Cotton of Calcutta (1813–66).

XVII. QUEEN AND COUNTRY

The Saints of our own land

GOD, whom the glorious companies of the
redeemed adore, assembled from all times
and places of Thy dominion: We praise Thee for
the saints of our own land who stand before Thee,
and for the many lamps their holiness hath lit;
and beseech Thee that we also may be numbered
at the last with them that have done Thy will and
declared Thy righteousness; through Jesus Christ
our Lord. *Amen.*

Memorials (based on a prayer of Dr. Alexander Nairne,
1862–1936).

Reconstruction

GRANT, O merciful God, that with malice
toward none, with charity to all, with firm-
ness in the right as Thou givest us to see the right,
we may strive to finish the work we are in; to bind
up the nation's wounds; to care for him who shall
have borne the battle and for his widow and his

orphan; to do all which may achieve and cherish a just and lasting peace among ourselves and with all nations; through Jesus Christ our Lord. *Amen.*

From the speech of Abraham Lincoln at his second inauguration as President, 4 March 1865.

XVIII–XIX. THE COMMONWEALTH AND THE WHOLE WORLD

O GOD our Father, and Father of all men, from whom all come, to whom all at last return: Bind together Thy children everywhere with the bond of mutual love, that they may claim in Thee their common birthright, and find in Thee their common service; through Jesus Christ our Lord. *Amen.*

XX. ALL WORKERS

The Spirit of freedom

O GOD, renew our spirits by Thy Holy Spirit, and draw our hearts unto Thyself, that our work may be not a burden, but a delight. Let us not serve as slaves with the spirit of bondage, but with freedom and gladness as Thy sons, rejoicing in Thy will; for Jesus Christ's sake. *Amen.*

Benjamin Jenks (1646–1724).

Duty

GOD, who hast made every calling of man acceptable to Thyself, if only Thy glory be intended in it: Give us day by day the desire to do our work, of what sort soever it be, for Thine honour; and the joy of rendering it to Thee well done; through Jesus Christ our Lord. *Amen.*

Memorials.

Jesus the Carpenter

ALMIGHTY God, who didst ordain that Thy
Son, Jesus Christ, should labour with His
hands to supply His own needs, and the needs of
others: Teach us, we pray Thee, that no labour is
mean, and all labour is divine, to which Thou dost
call us; to the glory of Thy holy Name: through
the same Jesus Christ our Lord. *Amen.*

For all men, all classes, all peoples

O LORD, teach us our need of one another:
make us remember how much we owe to one
another: and fill us with a desire to help one
another. For Jesus Christ's sake. *Amen.*

XXI. THE QUEEN'S FORCES

Before a War Memorial

O LORD our God, whose name only is excellent and Thy praise above heaven and
earth: We give Thee high praise and hearty
thanks for all those who counted not their lives
dear unto themselves but laid them down for their
friends; beseeching Thee to give them a part and
a lot in those good things which Thou hast prepared for all those whose names are written in the
Book of Life; and grant to us, that having them
always in remembrance, we may imitate their
faithfulness and with them inherit the new name
which Thou hast promised to them that over-
come; through Jesus Christ our Lord. *Amen.*

Frank Edward Brightman (1856–1932).

XXII. For those at Sea

O GOD, the Saviour of the world, we beseech
Thee, for the Passion of Christ, to have us
in Thy keeping. Help us in danger never to
despair, for Thou wilt defend and preserve us,
and bring us to our desired haven; to whom be
all honour, glory and praise, for ever and ever.
Amen.   *Sir Francis Drake (c. 1540–96),*
slightly adapted from a letter written to his little fleet
in the seas of New Spain, at a time of great peril.
Drake being then in the Golden Hind—*formerly*
the Pelican.

XXIII. All who Travel by Air

O FATHER of lights, with whom there is no
variableness, nor shadow of turning: who
abidest steadfast as the stars of heaven: Give us
grace to rest upon Thy eternal changelessness,
and in Thy faithfulness find peace; through Jesus
Christ our Lord. *Amen.*

XXIV. The School

LET Thy blessing, O Lord, rest upon our work
this day. Teach us to seek after truth, and
enable us to attain it; but grant that as we increase
in the knowledge of earthly things, we may grow
in the knowledge of Thee, whom to know is life
eternal; through Jesus Christ our Lord. *Amen.*

Adapted from Thomas Arnold (1795–1842),
Headmaster of Rugby.

Friendship

LORD, who hast provided for us many friends,
giving to us freely and without thought of
return: Grant that we, remembering that we are

debtors, may render to others the kindnesses which we ourselves have received; for Jesus Christ's sake. *Amen.*

Benefactors

O GOD our Father, who hast raised up for us many benefactors, known and unknown, remembered and forgotten, whose harvest we to-day are reaping: Make us also faithful in this our day, that we may sow a generous harvest, which others shall reap hereafter; through Jesus Christ our Lord. *Amen.*

Before the Bible Reading

O GRACIOUS God and most merciful Father, who hast vouchsafed us the rich and precious jewel of Thy holy Word: Assist us with Thy Spirit that it may be written in our hearts to our everlasting comfort, to reform us, to renew us according to Thine own image, to build us up, and edify us into the perfect building of Thy Christ, sanctifying and increasing in us all heavenly virtues. Grant this, O heavenly Father, for Jesus Christ's sake. *Amen.*

Preface to Geneva Bible, 1560.

XXV. CHRISTMAS
See Christian Year, p. 56.

XXVI. EASTER
See p. 57.

XXVII. ASCENSION
See p. 57.

XXVIII. Harvest

A General Thanksgiving

(may be said all together and on any occasion)

ALMIGHTY God, Father of all mercies, we Thine unworthy servants do give Thee most humble and hearty thanks for all Thy goodness and loving-kindness to us, and to all men. We bless Thee for our creation, preservation, and all the blessings of this life; but above all, for Thine inestimable love in the redemption of the world by our Lord Jesus Christ; for the means of grace, and for the hope of glory. And, we beseech Thee, give us that due sense of all Thy mercies, that our hearts may be unfeignedly thankful, and that we shew forth Thy praise, not only with our lips, but in our lives; by giving up ourselves to Thy service, and by walking before Thee in holiness and righteousness all our days; through Jesus Christ our Lord, to whom with Thee and the Holy Ghost be all honour and glory, world without end. *Amen.*   *Book of Common Prayer,* 1662.

XXIX and XXX. Adoration

BEFORE the glorious throne of Thy majesty, O Lord, and the awful judgment-seat of Thy burning love, we Thy people do kneel with cherubim and seraphim and archangels, worshipping, confessing, and praising Thee, Lord of all, Father, Son, and Holy Spirit for ever. *Amen.*

LORD God Almighty and All-merciful, whom angels and archangels worship, and all the host of heaven: In Thy loving-kindness accept the praises of Thy servants, though Thou art far beyond all that we can speak or think; through Him in whom Thy love has been made manifest to us, Jesus Christ Thy Son our Lord. *Amen.*

THE CHRISTIAN YEAR

The Coming of the Kingdom
(Advent)

O GOD, who hast sent Thy servants to prepare Thy way: Fill our hearts with love, and strengthen our hands to work, that we may make ready the way of our King. For Jesus Christ's sake. *Amen.*

Christmastide

GRANT, heavenly Father, that as we keep the birthday of Jesus, He may be born again in our hearts; that we may grow in the likeness of the Son of God, who for our sake was born the Son of man: through the same Jesus Christ our Lord. *Amen.*

The Light of the World
(Epiphany)

ALMIGHTY and Everlasting God, the brightness of faithful souls, who didst bring the Gentiles to Thy light, and madest known unto them Him who is the true Light and the bright and morning Star; Fill, we beseech Thee, the world with Thy glory, and shew Thyself by the radiance of Thy light unto all nations; through Jesus Christ our Lord. *Amen.*

Book of Worship for Youth: based on an ancient collect.

Lent

ALMIGHTY God, who seest that we have no power of ourselves to help ourselves; Keep us both outwardly in our bodies, and inwardly in our souls; that we may be defended from all adversities which may happen to the body, and from all evil thoughts which may assault and hurt the soul; through Jesus Christ our Lord. *Amen.*

Book of Common Prayer, 1549.

Holy Week

ALMIGHTY God, we beseech Thee graciously to behold this Thy family, for which our Lord Jesus Christ was contented to be betrayed, and given up into the hands of wicked men, and to suffer death upon the cross, who now liveth and reigneth with Thee and the Holy Ghost, ever one God, world without end. *Amen.* *Ancient.*

Eastertide

O GOD, the living God, who hast given unto us a living hope by the resurrection of Jesus Christ from the dead: Grant that we, being risen with Him, may seek the things which are above, and be made partakers of the life eternal; through the same Jesus Christ our Lord. *Amen.*

Ascension

O GOD the King of glory, who hast exalted Thine only Son Jesus Christ with great triumph unto Thy kingdom in heaven; We beseech Thee, leave us not comfortless; but send to us Thine Holy Ghost to comfort us, and exalt us unto the same place whither our Saviour Christ is gone before, who liveth and reigneth with Thee and the Holy Ghost, one God, world without end. *Amen.* *From the Latin of the Sarum Breviary.*

Whitsuntide

GOD, who didst give Thy Holy Spirit to guide and strengthen Thy faithful people, and to bind them into one fellowship; Fill us now with the same Spirit, that our hearts may be all on fire to love Thee: and loving Thee, to love one another. Through Jesus Christ our Lord. *Amen.*

All Saints

O ALMIGHTY God, who hast knit together Thine elect in one communion and fellowship, in the mystical body of Thy Son Christ our Lord: Grant us grace so to follow Thy blessed Saints in all virtuous and godly living, that we may come to those unspeakable joys, which Thou hast prepared for them that unfeignedly love Thee; through Jesus Christ our Lord. *Amen.*

Book of Common Prayer, 1549.

EVENING PRAYERS

(Since most schools have Morning, and not Evening, Assembly, no series of Evening Services has been thought necessary. But most of the preceding are equally suitable for Evening Prayer; and a few special prayers are here added.)

LIGHTEN our darkness, we beseech Thee, O Lord: and by Thy great mercy defend us from all perils and dangers of this night: for the love of Thy only Son, our Saviour, Jesus Christ. *Amen.* *5th century.*

SAVE us, O Lord, waking; guard us sleeping; that awake we may watch with Christ, and asleep we may rest in peace. *Amen.*

An evening thanksgiving

> Let us give thanks,
> For friends and home,
> For work and play,
> For hands to make, and eyes to see, and lips
>   to speak;
> For strength to do each daily task,
> And, at the end, the gift of quiet sleep.
>
> *Amen.*

I will lay me down in peace, and sleep:
>   for Thou, Lord, only makest me dwell in
>   safety.   *Psalm 4.*

THE LORD'S PRAYER

NOTE. *Musical settings of The Lord's Prayer will be found in the Full Music and Melody Editions of 'The Daily Service'.*

THE DOXOLOGIES OF SCRIPTURE

BLESSING, and honour, and glory, and power be unto Him that sitteth upon the throne, and unto the Lamb for ever and ever. *Amen.*

NOW unto Him that is able to keep you from falling, and to present you faultless before the presence of His glory with exceeding joy,
   To the only wise God our Saviour, be glory and majesty, dominion and power, both now and ever. *Amen.*

NOW unto Him that is able to do exceeding abundantly above all that we ask or think, according to the power that worketh in us,
   Unto Him be glory in the Church by Christ Jesus throughout all ages, world without end. *Amen.*

TO God, the blessed and only Potentate,
      King of kings, and Lord of lords:
Who only hath immortality, dwelling in
   The light which no man can approach unto;
Whom no man hath seen, nor can see:
   To Him be honour and power everlasting.
                                             Amen.

See also p. 1. Now unto the King eternal.
          p. 19. Unto Him that loved us.
          p. 36. Now the God of Peace.

HYMNS OF THE BIBLE

I. The Old Testament

The Psalter was the hymn-book of the Jewish Church: and therefore our Lord's hymn-book.

The text is primarily that of the Great Bible of 1539, with its musical cadences: but there are some corrections from A.V. of 1611, and R.V., completed in 1885, for improvement of rhythm or greater accuracy. Details will be found in the full-music edition.

Chanting should be, as far as possible, in the free rhythm of natural speech.

Psalm 1—*The Two Ways*

BLESSED is the man that hath not walked in the counsel of the ungodly, * nor stood in the | way of | sinners : and hath not | sat · in the | seat · of the | scornful.

2 But his delíght is in the | law · of the | Lord : and in his láw doth he | meditate | day and | night.

3 And he shall be like a tree plánted by the | water- | side : that will bring fórth his | fruit in | due — | season.

4 His léaf also | shall not | wither : and look, whatsoever he | do-eth | it shall | prosper.

5 As for the ungodly, it is nót | so with | them : but they are like the chaff which the wind scáttereth a- | way · from the | face · of the | earth.

6 Therefore the ungodly shall not be áble to | stand · in the | judgement : neither the sinners in the congre- | ga-tion | of the | righteous.

[*2nd part*] 7 But the Lord knóweth the | way · of the | righteous : and the | way of · the un- | godly · shall | perish.

Psalm 15—*God's Guest*

LORD, whó shall | dwell in · thy | tabernacle :
or who shall | rest up-on thy | ho-ly | hill?

2 Even he that leadeth an | uncor-rupt | life :
and doeth the thing which is right, and spéaketh
the | truth — | from his | heart.

3 He that hath used no deceit in his tongue, *
nor done | evil · to his | neighbour : and | hath
not | slandered · his | neighbour.

4 In whose eyes a vile person | is de- | spised :
but he hónoureth | them that | fear the | Lord.

5 He that sweareth unto his neighbour, and
disap- | pointeth · him | not : though it | were · to
his | own — | hindrance.

6 He that putteth not out his | money · to |
usury : nor táketh re- | ward a- | gainst the |
innocent.

7 Whóso | doeth these | things : shall | nev — |
— er | fall.

Psalm 19—*The Outward Law*

THE heavens decláre the | glory · of | God :
and the | firma-ment | sheweth · his | handy-
work.

2 One dáy | telleth · an- | other : and one níght |
cer-ti- | fieth · an- | other.

3 There is no | speech nor | language : their |
voice can- | not be | heard.

4 *Yet* their sound is gone óut into | all — |
lands : and their wórds into the | ends — | of the |
world.

5 In them hath he set a tábernacle | for the |
sun : which cometh forth as a bridegroom out of
his chamber, * and rejóiceth as a | strong · man
to | run a | race.

6 It goeth forth from the uttermost part of the heaven, * and runneth about unto the énd of | it a- | gain : and there is nothing | hid · from the | heat there- | of.

The Inward Law

[2nd chant]

7 The law of the Lord is an undefiled láw * con- | verting · the | soul : the testimony of the Lord is sure, * and giveth | wis-dom | unto · the | simple.

8 The statutes of the Lord are ríght, and re- | joice the | heart : the commandment of the Lord is pure, * and gíveth | light — | unto · the | eyes.

9 The fear of the Lord is cléan and en- | dureth · for | ever : the judgements of the Lord are trúe, and | righteous | al-to- | gether.

10 More to be desired are they than gold, yéa than | much fine | gold : sweeter also than | hon-ey, | and the | honey-comb.

11 Moreover by thém is thy | serv-ant | taught : and in kéeping of them | there is | great re- | ward.

[3rd chant]

12 Who can tell how | oft · he of- | fendeth : O cléanse thou me | from my | se-cret | faults.

13 Keep thy servant also from presumptuous sins, * lest they get the do- | min-ion | over me : so shall I be undefiled, * and ínnocent | from the | great of- | fence.

14 Let the words of my mouth, * and the meditation of my heart, * be alway accéptable | in thy | sight : O Lórd my | strength and | my re- | deemer.   [*Gloria to* 1st chant.]

Psalm 23

THE Lórd | is my | shepherd : therefore | can
I | lack — | nothing.

2 He shall féed me in a | green — | pasture :
and lead me forth be- | side the | waters · of |
comfort.

3 Hé shall con- | vert my | soul : and bring me
forth in the páths of | righteous-ness | for his |
Name's sake.

4 Yea though I walk through the valley of
the shadow of death, * I will | fear no | evil : for
thóu art with me, * thy ród and thy | staff — |
comfort | me.

5 Thou shalt prepare a table before me, *
against | them that | trouble me : thou hast
anointed my head with oíl, | and my | cup · shall
be | full.

6 But thy loving-kindness and mercy shall
follow me, * áll the | days of · my | life : and I
will dwéll in the | house · of the | Lord for | ever.

Psalm 24—*The Palace of the King of Glory*

THE earth is the Lord's, and all that | therein |
is : the compass of the wórld · and | they that |
dwell there- | in.

2 For he hath fóunded it up- | on the | seas :
and pre- | pared · it up- | on the | floods.

3 Who shall ascénd into the | hill · of the |
Lord : or who shall | stand · in his | holy | place?

4 Even he that hath clean hánds and a | pure — |
heart : and that hath not lift up his mind unto
vanity, * nor | sworn · to de- | ceive his | neighbour.

5 He shall recéive the | blessing · from the |
Lord : and ríghteousness from the | God of | his
sal- | vation.

6 This is the generation of | them that | seek
him : even of them that | seek thy | face O |
Jacob.

[2nd chant]

7 Lift up your heads O ye gates, * and be ye
lift úp ye ever- | last-ing | doors : and the King
of | glo-ry | shall come | in.

8 Whó is the | King of | glory : it is the Lord
strong and mighty, * even the | Lord — | mighty ·
in | battle.

9 Lift up your heads O ye gates, * and be ye lift
úp ye ever- | last-ing | doors : and the Kíng of |
glo-ry | shall come | in.

10. Whó is the | King of | glory : even the Lord
of hósts, | he · is the | King of | glory.

(NOTE.—This is a Dedication-psalm, with almost certain
reference to the Temple.)

Psalm 46

[Verses 7 and 11 (only) to 2nd chant.]

GÓD is our | refuge · and | strength : a very |
pre-sent | help in | trouble.

2 Therefore will we not féar though the | earth
be | mov'd : and though the hills be carried |
into · the | midst · of the | sea.

3 Though the waters thereof | rage and | swell :
and though the mountains sháke at the | tempest |
of the | same.

4 The rivers of the flood thereof shall make
glád the | city · of | God : the holy place of the
tábernacles | of the | Most — | High.

5 God is in the midst of her, * thérefore shall
she | not · be re- | moved : Gód shall | help her, ·
and | that right | early.

6 The nations make much ado, and the | king-
doms · are | moved : but God hath shewed his
voice, and the | earth shall | melt a- | way.

7 *The Lórd of | hosts is | with us : the Gód of |
Ja-cob | is our | refuge.*

8 O come hither and behold the | works · of
the | Lord : what destrúction he hath | brought
up- | on the | earth.

9 He maketh wars to cease in | all the | world :
he breaketh the bow, and knappeth the spear in
sunder, ★ and búrneth the | chariots | in the | fire.

10 Be still then and knów that | I am | God :
I will be exalted among the nations, ★ and I will
be ex- | alt-ed | in the | earth.

11 *The Lórd of | hosts is | with us : the Gód of |
Ja-cob | is our | refuge.*

Psalm 51—*A Clean Heart*

[*Some verses omitted.*]

HAVE mercy upon me, O God, ★ after thy |
great — | goodness : according to the multi-
tude of thy mercies, | do a-way | mine of- | fences.

2 Wash me thróughly | from my | wickedness :
and | cleanse me | from my | sin.

3 For I ac- | knowledge · my | faults : and my |
sin is | ever · be- | fore me.

4 Against thée only | have I | sinned : and done
this | ev-il | in thy | sight.

7 Thou shalt purge me with hyssop, and | I
shall · be | clean : thou shalt wash me, and | I shall ·
be | whiter · than | snow.

9 Túrn thy face | from my | sins : and | put
out | all · my mis- | deeds.

10 Make me a cléan | heart, O | God : and re- |
new a · right | spirit · with- | in me.

[2nd chant]

15 O Lord, ópen | thou my | lips : and my
móuth | shall shew | forth thy | praise.

16 For thou desireth no sacrifice, | else · would
I | give it thee : but thou delíghtest | not in |
burnt — | offerings.

17 The sacrifice of God is a | troubled | spirit :
a broken and contrite heart, O Gód, | shalt thou |
not de- | spise.   [Gloria to 2nd chant.]

Psalm 65

THOU O Gód art | praised in | Sion : and unto
thee shall the vów be per- | formed — | in
Je- | rusalem.

2 O thóu that | hearest | prayer : unto | thee
shall | all flesh | come.

3 My misdéeds pre- | vail a- | gainst me : O be
thou | merci-ful | unto · our | sins.

4 Blessed is the man whom thou choosest, and
recéivest | un-to | thee : he shall dwell in thy
court, * and shall be satisfied with the pleasures
of thy house, * éven | of thy | ho-ly | temple.

5 Thou shalt shew us wonderful things in thy
righteousness, O Gód of | our salv- | ation : thou
that art the hope of all the ends of the earth, and
of them that re- | main · in the | broad — | sea.

6 Who in his stréngth setteth | fast the | moun-
tains : and is | girded · a- | bout with | power.

7 Who stílleth the | raging · of the | sea : and
the noise of his wáves, and the | tumult | of the |
peoples.

8 They also that dwell in the uttermost parts
of the éarth shall be a- | fraid at · thy | tokens :
thou that makest the outgoings of the | morning ·
and | evening · to | praise thee.

9 Thou vísitest the | earth and | blessest it : thou | makest · it | ve-ry | plenteous.

10 The river of Gód is | full of | water : thou preparest their corn, for só thou pro- | vid-est | for the | earth.

11 Thou waterest her furrows, thou sendest rain into the little | valleys · there- | of : thou makest it soft with the drops of rain, and | blessest · the | in-crease | of it.

12 Thou crownest the yéar | with thy | good- ness : and thy | clouds — | drop — | fatness.

13 They shall dróp upon the | pastures · of the | wilderness : and the little hílls shall re- | joice on | ever-y | side.

14 The fólds shall be | full of | sheep : the valleys also shall stand so thick with córn, that | they shall | laugh and | sing.

Psalm 98—*A Missionary Psalm*

O SÍNG unto the Lórd a | new — | song : for | he hath · done | marvel-lous | things.

2 With his own right hand, and with his | ho-ly | arm : hath he | gotten · him- | self the | victory.

3 The Lord decláred | his salv- | ation : his righteousness hath he ópenly | shewed · in the | sight · of the | nations.

4 He hath remembered his mercy and truth toward the | house of | Israel : and all the ends of the world have séen the salv- | a-tion | of our | God.

5 Shew yourselves joyful unto the Lórd | all ye | lands : síng, re- | joice and | give — | thanks.

6 Praise the Lórd up- | on the | harp : síng to the | harp · with a | psalm of | thanksgiving.

7 With trúmpets | also · and | shawms : O shew
yourselves jóyful be- | fore the | Lord the | King.

8 Let the sea make a noise, ★ and áll that |
there-in | is : the round wórld and | they that |
dwell there- | in.

9 Let the floods clap their hands, ★ and let the
hills be joyful togéther be- | fore the | Lord : for
he | cometh · to | judge the | earth.

10 With ríghteousness | shall he | judge : the |
world · and the | peoples · with | equity.

Psalm 103—*The Everlasting Mercy*

Pᴿᴬᴵˢᴱ the Lórd | O my | soul : and all that is
within me | praise his | ho-ly | Name.

2 Praise the Lórd | O my | soul : and for- | get
not | all his | benefits;

3 Who forgíveth | all thy | sin : and | heal-eth |
all · thine in- | firmities;

4 Who saveth thy life | from de- | struction :
and crówneth thee with | mercy · and | lov-ing- |
kindness;

[*2nd part*] 5 Who satisfieth thy móuth with |
good — | things : so that thy yóuth is re- | newed
— | like the | eagle.

6 The Lord executeth | righteous-ness and |
judgement : for all | them that · are op- | pressed
with | wrong.

7 He shéwed his | ways un-to | Moses : his
wórks | unto · the | children · of | Israel.

8 The Lord is fúll of com- | passion · and |
mercy : long-súffering | and of | great — | good-
ness.

9 He will not | alway · be | chiding : neither |
keepeth · he his | anger · for | ever.

[*2nd part*] 10 He hath not deált with us |

after · our | sins : nor rewárded us ac- | cord-ing | to our | wickednesses.

11 For look how high the héaven is in com- | parison · of the | earth : so great is his mércy also | toward — | them that | fear him.

12 Look how wide also the eást is | from the | west : so fár hath he | set our | sins — | from us.

13 Yea, like as a father pítieth his | own — | children : even so is the Lord mérciful | unto | them that | fear him.

14 For he knóweth where- | of · we are | made : he re- | membereth · that | we are · but | dust.

15 The days of mán are | but as | grass : for he flóurisheth as a | flow-er | of the | field.

16 For as soon as the wind goeth óver it, | it is | gone : and the | place there-of shall | know it · no | more.

17 But the merciful goodness of the Lord, ★ endureth for ever and éver upon | them that | fear him : and his | righteous-ness upon | children's | children;

18 Even upon súch as | keep his | covenant : and thínk upon | his com- | mandments · to | do them.

19 The Lord hath estáblished his | throne · in the | heavens : and his kingdom | rul-eth | ov-er | all.

20 O praise the Lord ye angels of his, ★ yé that ex- | cel in | strength : ye that fulfil his commandment, ★ and héarken | unto · the | voice of · his | words.

21 O praise the Lórd, all | ye his | hosts : ye servants of | his that | do his | pleasure.

22 O speak good of the Lord all ye works of his, ★ in all pláces of | his do- | minion : praíse thou the | Lord — | O my | soul.

Psalm 121

I WILL lift up mine éyes | unto · the | hills. ⋆
From | whence — | cometh · my | help?

2 My help cometh even | from the | Lord :
who hath | made — | heaven and | earth.

3 He will not súffer thy | foot · to be | mov'd :
and he that | keepeth · thee | will not | sleep.

4 Behold, hé that | keep-eth | Israel : shall |
nei-ther | slumber · nor | sleep.

5 The Lórd him- | self · is thy | keeper : the
Lord is thy sháde up- | on thy | right — | hand;

6 So that the sún shall not | burn thee · by |
day : nei- | ther the | moon by | night.

7 The Lord shall presérve thee from | all — |
evil : yea it is even hé | that shall | keep thy | soul.

8 The Lord shall preserve thy going óut, and
thy | com-ing | in : from thís time | forth for |
ev-er- | more.

Psalm 122—*A Pilgrim Song*

I WAS gláde when they | said · unto | me : we
will | go in-to the | house · of the | Lord.

2 Our | feet shall | stand : in thy | gates — | O
Je- | rusalem.

3 Jerusalem is | built · as a | city : that is at |
unity | in it- | self.

4 For thither the tribes go up, ⋆ éven the |
tribes · of the | Lord : to testify unto Israel, to
give thánks | unto the | Name · of the | Lord.

5 For thére is the | seat of | judgement : éven
the | seat · of the | house of | David.

6 O práy for the | peace · of Je- | rusalem :
théy shall | prosper · that | love — | thee.

7 Péace be with- | in thy | walls : and | plen-
teous-ness with- | in thy | palaces.

8 For my bréthren and com- | panions' | sakes : I will | wish — | thee pros- | perity.

[*2nd part*] 9 Yea, because of the hóuse of the | Lord our | God : I will | seek to | do thee | good.

Psalm 126—*A Song of Deliverance*

WHEN the Lord turned agaín the cap- | tivi-ty of | Sion : then were we | like · unto | them that | dream.

2 Then was our móuth | filled with | laughter : and our | tongue — | with — | joy.

3 Then said they a- | mong the | nations : the Lórd hath | done great | things for | them.

4 Yea, the Lord hath done great thíngs for | us al- | ready : where- | of — | we re- | joice.

5 Túrn our cap- | tivi-ty, O | Lord : as the | riv-ers | in the | south.

6 Théy that | sow in | tears : shall | reap — | in — | joy.

[*2nd part*] 7 He that now goeth on his way weeping, and béareth | forth good | seed : shall doubtless come again with jóy, and | bring his | sheaves — | with him.

Psalm 150—*A Song of Universal Praise*

O PRAISE Gód | in his | holiness : práise him in the | firma-ment | of his | power.

2 Práise him in his | no-ble | acts : práise him ac- | cording · to his | excel-lent | greatness.

3 Práise him in the | sound · of the | trumpet : práise him up- | on the | lute and | harp.

4 Práise him in the | cymbals · and | dances : práise him up- | on the | strings and | pipe.

5 Praise him upón the | well-tuned | cymbals : praise him up- | on the | loud — | cymbals.

6 Let éverything | that hath | breath : praise |
— | — the | Lord.

II. The New Testament

The Song of Zacharias—BENEDICTUS

(*St. Luke* 1. 68)

BLÉSSED be the | Lord · God of | Israel : for he
hath vísited | and re- | deemed his | people;

2 And hath raised up a mighty salv- | a-tion ·
for us : in the | house of · his | serv-ant | David;

3 As he spake by the móuth of his | ho-ly |
Prophets : which have been | since the | world
be- | gan;

4 That we should be | saved · from our | ene-
mies : and from the | hands of | all that | hate us;

5 To perform the mércy | promised · to our |
forefathers : and to re- | member · his | ho-ly |
Covenant;

6 To perform the oath which he swáre to our |
forefather | Abraham : that | he would | give
— | us;

7 That we being delivered out of the | hand ·
of our | enemies : might | serve · him with- |
out — | fear;

8 In hóliness and | righteous-ness be- | fore
him : all the | days — | of our | life.

9 And thou child shalt be called the | Prophet ·
of the | Highest : * for thou shalt go before the
face of the Lórd | to pre- | pare his | ways;

10 To give knowledge of salvátion | unto · his |
people : for the re- | mis-sion | of their | sins;

11 Through the tender mércy of | our — |
God : whereby the dáyspring from on | high
hath | visit-ed | us.

12 To give light to them that sit in darkness, *
and in the | shadow · of | death : and to guide our
féet | into the | way of | peace.

Glóry | be · to the | Father : and to the Són, |
and · to the | Ho-ly | Ghost;

As it was in the beginning, is nów, and | ever |
shall be : world without | end. A- | — | men.

The Song of Mary—MAGNIFICAT

(St. Luke 1. 46)

M Y sóul doth | magni-fy the | Lord : and my
spírit hath re- | joiced in | God my | Saviour.

2 For | he hath · re- | garded : the | lowli-ness |
of his | hand-maiden.

3 For be- | hold from | henceforth : áll gener- |
ations · shall | call me | blessed.

4 For he that is míghty hath | magni-fied | me :
and | ho-ly | is his | Name.

[2nd part] 5 And his mércy is on | them that |
fear him : throughout | all — | gen-er- | ations.

6 He hath shéwed | strength · with his | arm :
he hath scattered the próud in the imágin- |
a-tion | of their | hearts.

7 He hath put down the mighty | from their |
seat : and hath ex- | alted · the | humble · and | meek.

8 He hath filled the húngry with | good — |
things : and the rich he hath | sent — | empty ·
a- | way.

9 He remembering his mercy hath hólpen his |
serv-ant | Israel : as he promised to our fore-
fathers, * Abraham | and his | seed for | ever.

Glóry | be · to the | Father : and to the Són, |
and · to the | Ho-ly | Ghost;

As it was in the beginning, is nów, and | ever |
shall be : world without | end. A- | — | men.

The Song of Simeon—NUNC DIMITTIS
(St. Luke 2. 29)

LORD, now lettest thou thy sérvant de- | part
in | peace : ac- | cord-ing | to thy | word.

2 For mine éyes have | seen · thy salv- | ation :
which thou hast prepáred before the | face of |
all — | people;

3 To be a light to | lighten · the | Gentiles :
and to be the | glory · of thy | peo-ple | Israel.

Glóry | be · to the | Father : and to the Són, |
and · to the | Ho-ly | Ghost;

As it was in the beginning, is nów, and | ever |
shall be : world without | end. A- | — | men.

HYMNS

ACKNOWLEDGEMENTS

THANKS are due to the following copyright owners for permission to include words of hymns:

WORDS OF HYMNS

Very Rev. C. A. Alington, 63; Sir J. S. Arkwright, 171; Mr. H. N. Brailsford, 18; Mrs. Bridges and the Oxford University Press, 70, 120, 157 (each from *The Yattendon Hymnal*); Rev. Canon G. W. Briggs, 9, 22, 30, 93, 106, 161, Grace 1; Mr. H. Brooke, 33; Mrs. Burkitt, 67; Messrs. J. Curwen & Sons, Ltd., 16 (from Curwen Edition No. 6333); Rev. L. J. T. Darwall, Carol 6; Rev. Dr. Dearmer, 37, 80, 89, 125, 140; Miss Eleanor Farjeon, 147; Mr. Frank Fletcher, 40; Mr. William Galbraith, 6; Mr. Norman Gale, 73; Miss Hatch, 88; Mr. R. Holland (National Society's Graded Hymnbook), 158; Messrs. Houghton Mifflin Co., 76; Mr. Laurence Housman, 51; Mr. F. D. How, 108; the late Mr. Rudyard Kipling, 165 (from *Puck of Pook's Hill*, published by Messrs. Macmillan & Co., Ltd.), 167 (from *The Five Nations*, published by Messrs. Methuen & Co., Ltd.); Mrs. E. Rutter Leatham, Grace 2; Messrs. Longmans, Green & Co., Ltd., 168; Headmaster of Loughborough Grammar School and Headmistress of Loughborough High School, 162; Mr. Basil Mathews, 135; Estate of the late Mr. Thomas Bird Mosher, 114; Mrs. Myers, 82; Oxford University Press, 2, 6, 9, 13, 19, 20, 22, 30, 33, 36, 37, 40, 42, 43, 45, 74, 80, 89, 93, 106, 117, 119, 125, 134, 140, 161; Carols 2, 3, 8, 9; Rev. E. Pelham Pierpoint, 113; Rev. W. Charter Piggott, 71, 77, 98; Miss Pott, 64; Messrs. A. W. Ridley & Co., 87, 139, 153; Mr. W. H. C. Romanis, 154; Messrs. Skeffington & Son, Ltd., 171; Society for Promoting Christian Knowledge, 67; Jan Struther, 54, 79, 107, 112, 116, 143, Carol 10; Lady Spring Rice, 168; Mr. L. G. P. Thring, 136. We also acknowledge the copyright hymns marked *Songs of Praise version*; also the centos and versions marked † or ‡.

CONTENTS

GOD OUR FATHER

1 *Ps.* 100. *W. Kethe, Day's Psalter* (1560–1).

ALL people that on earth do dwell,
   Sing to the Lord with cheerful voice;
Him serve with mirth, his praise forth tell,
   Come ye before him, and rejoice.

2 The Lord, ye know, is God indeed,
   Without our aid he did us make;
We are his folk, he doth us feed,
   And for his sheep he doth us take.

3 O enter then his gates with praise,
   Approach with joy his courts unto;
Praise, laud, and bless his name always,
   For it is seemly so to do.

4 For why? the Lord our God is good:
   His mercy is for ever sure,
His truth at all times firmly stood,
   And shall from age to age endure.

5 To Father, Son, and Holy Ghost,
   The God whom heaven and earth adore,
From men and from the angel-host
   Be praise and glory evermore.

2 *From Goethe. P. Dearmer,* 1867–1936.

EVERYTHING changes,
   But God changes not;
The power never changes
   That lies in his thought:
Splendours three, from God proceeding,
   May we ever love them true,
Goodness, Truth, and Beauty heeding
   Every day, in all we do.

2 Truth never changes,
   And Beauty's her dress,
And Good never changes,
   Which those two express:

3 Perfect together
   And lovely apart,
These three cannot wither;
   They spring from God's heart:

4 Some things are screening
   God's glory below;
But this is the meaning
   Of all that we know:

3   *W. Cowper*, 1731–1800.

GOD moves in a mysterious way
   His wonders to perform;
He plants his footsteps in the sea,
   And rides upon the storm.

2 Deep in unfathomable mines
   Of never-failing skill
He treasures up his bright designs,
   And works his sovereign will.

3 Ye fearful saints, fresh courage take,
   The clouds ye so much dread
Are big with mercy, and shall break
   In blessings on your head.

4 Judge not the Lord by feeble sense,
   But trust him for his grace;
Behind a frowning providence
   He hides a smiling face.

5 His purposes will ripen fast,
   Unfolding every hour;
The bud may have a bitter taste,
   But sweet will be the flower.

6 Blind unbelief is sure to err,
   And scan his work in vain;
God is his own interpreter,
   And he will make it plain.

4　　　　　　　　　　*Bishop R. Heber*, 1783–1826.

HOLY, Holy, Holy! Lord God Almighty!
　　Early in the morning our song shall rise to thee;
Holy, Holy, Holy! Merciful and mighty!
　　God in three Persons, blessèd Trinity!

2 Holy, Holy, Holy! all the Saints adore thee,
　　　Casting down their golden crowns around the
　　　　　glassy sea;
　Cherubim and Seraphim falling down before thee,
　　Which wert, and art, and evermore shalt be.

3 Holy, Holy, Holy! though the darkness hide thee,
　　　Though the eye of sinful man thy glory may not
　　　　　see,
　Only thou art holy, there is none beside thee
　　Perfect in power, in love, and purity.

4 Holy, Holy, Holy! Lord God Almighty!
　　　All thy works shall praise thy name, in earth, and
　　　　　sky, and sea;
　Holy, Holy, Holy! Merciful and mighty!
　　God in three Persons, blessèd Trinity!

5　　　　　　　　　　*John Mason, c.* 1645–94.

HOW shall I sing that Majesty
　　Which angels do admire?
Let dust in dust and silence lie;
　　Sing, sing, ye heavenly choir.
Thousands of thousands stand around
　　Thy throne, O God most high;
Ten thousand times ten thousand sound
　　Thy praise; but who am I?

2 Thy brightness unto them appears,
　　　Whilst I thy footsteps trace;
　A sound of God comes to my ears,
　　　But they behold thy face.
　They sing because thou art their Sun;
　　　Lord, send a beam on me;
　For where heaven is but once begun
　　　There Alleluyas be.

3 Enlighten with faith's light my heart,
　Inflame it with love's fire;
Then shall I sing and bear a part
　With that celestial choir.
I shall, I fear, be dark and cold,
　With all my fire and light;
Yet when thou dost accept their gold,
　Lord, treasure up my mite.

4 How great a being, Lord, is thine,
　Which doth all beings keep!
Thy knowledge is the only line
　To sound so vast a deep.
Thou art a sea without a shore,
　A sun without a sphere;
Thy time is now and evermore,
　Thy place is everywhere.

6　　　　　　　　*W. Chalmers Smith*, 1824-1908.

IMMORTAL, invisible, God only wise,
　In light inaccessible hid from our eyes,
Most blessed, most glorious, the Ancient of Days,
Almighty, victorious, thy great name we praise.

2 Unresting, unhasting, and silent as light,
Nor wanting, nor wasting, thou rulest in might;
Thy justice like mountains high soaring above
Thy clouds which are fountains of goodness and
　　love.

3 To all life thou givest—to both great and small;
In all life thou livest, the true life of all;
We blossom and flourish as leaves on the tree,
And wither and perish—but nought changeth thee.

4 Great Father of glory, pure Father of light,
Thine Angels adore thee, all veiling their sight;
All laud we would render: O help us to see
'Tis only the splendour of light hideth thee.

GOD OUR FATHER

7

O. Wendell Holmes, 1809–94.

LORD of all being, throned afar,
  Thy glory flames from sun and star;
Centre and soul of every sphere,
Yet to each loving heart how near!

2 Sun of our life, thy quickening ray
Sheds on our path the glow of day;
Star of our hope, thy softened light
Cheers the long watches of the night.

3 Our midnight is thy smile withdrawn,
Our noontide is thy gracious dawn,
Our rainbow arch thy mercy's sign;
All, save the clouds of sin, are thine.

4 Lord of all life, below, above,
Whose light is truth, whose warmth is love,
Before thy ever-blazing throne
We ask no lustre of our own.

5 Grant us thy truth to make us free
And kindling hearts that burn for thee,
Till all thy living altars claim
One holy light, one heavenly flame.

8

F. W. Faber,‡ 1814–63.

MY God, how wonderful thou art,
  Thy majesty how bright,
How beautiful thy mercy-seat,
  In depths of burning light!

2 How dread are thine eternal years,
  O everlasting Lord,
By shining spirits day and night
  Incessantly adored!

3 Yet I may love thee too, O Lord,
  Almighty as thou art,
For thou hast stooped to ask of me
  The love of my poor heart.

4 No earthly father loves like thee,
   No mother, e'er so mild,
Bears and forbears as thou hast done
   With me thy wilful child.

5 How wonderful, how beautiful,
   The sight of thee must be,
Thine endless wisdom, boundless power,
   And aweful purity!

9 *The Abiding Presence. G. W. Briggs,* 1875–1959.

O GOD, in whom we live and move,
   In whom we draw each breath,
Who fillest all the height above,
   And all the depths beneath;

2 Our hands may build thy hallowed fane,
   No bound thy presence owns;
The heaven of heavens cannot contain,
   The lowly heart enthrones.

3 Thou art about our path, where'er
   We seek to tread thy ways;
All life is sacrament and prayer,
   And every thought is praise.

10 *Ps.* 150.   *Sir H. W. Baker,* 1821–77.

O PRAISE ye the Lord!
   Praise him in the height;
Rejoice in his word,
   Ye angels of light;
Ye heavens adore him
   By whom ye were made,
And worship before him,
   In brightness arrayed.

2 O praise ye the Lord!
   Praise him upon earth,
In tuneful accord,
   Ye sons of new birth:

Praise him who hath brought you
    His grace from above,
Praise him who hath taught you
    To sing of his love.

3 O praise ye the Lord,
    All things that give sound;
Each jubilant chord,
    Re-echo around;
Loud organs, his glory
    Forth tell in deep tone,
And sweet harp, the story
    Of what he hath done.

4 O praise ye the Lord!
    Thanksgiving and song
To him be outpoured
    All ages along;
For love in creation,
    For heaven restored,
For grace of salvation,
    O praise ye the Lord!

11 *Ps.* 104.   *Sir R. Grant, 1785–1838.*

O WORSHIP the King
    All glorious above;
O gratefully sing
    His power and his love:
Our shield and defender,
    The Ancient of Days,
Pavilioned in splendour,
    And girded with praise.

2 O tell of his might,
    O sing of his grace,
Whose robe is the light,
    Whose canopy space.
His chariots of wrath
    The deep thunder-clouds form,
And dark is his path
    On the wings of the storm.

3 This earth, with its store
  Of wonders untold,
Almighty, thy power
  Hath founded of old:
Hath stablished it fast
  By a changeless decree,
And round it hath cast,
  Like a mantle, the sea.

4 Thy bountiful care
  What tongue can recite?
It breathes in the air,
  It shines in the light;
It streams from the hills,
  It descends to the plain,
And sweetly distils
  In the dew and the rain.

*5 Frail children of dust,
  And feeble as frail,
In thee do we trust,
  Nor find thee to fail;
Thy mercies how tender!
  How firm to the end!—
Our Maker, Defender,
  Redeemer, and Friend!

6 O measureless Might,
  Ineffable Love,
While angels delight
  To hymn thee above,
Thy humbler creation,
  Though feeble their lays,
With true adoration
  Shall sing to thy praise.

12 *Ps.* 148.   *Foundling Hospital Coll.* (1796).

PRAISE the Lord! ye heavens, adore him;
  Praise him, Angels, in the height;
Sun and moon, rejoice before him,
  Praise him, all ye stars and light:

Praise the Lord! for he hath spoken,
  Worlds his mighty voice obeyed;
Laws, which never shall be broken,
  For their guidance hath he made.

2 Praise the Lord! for he is glorious;
    Never shall his promise fail;
  God hath made his saints victorious,
    Sin and death shall not prevail.
  Praise the God of our salvation;
    Hosts on high, his power proclaim;
  Heaven and earth, and all creation,
    Laud and magnify his name!

13   *J. Neander, 1650–80. Tr. C. Winkworth.*‡

PRAISE to the Lord, the Almighty, the King of
    creation;
O my soul, praise him, for he is thy health and
    salvation:
    Come, ye who hear,
    Brothers and sisters, draw near,
Praise him in glad adoration.

2 Praise to the Lord, who o'er all things so won-
      drously reigneth,
  Shelters thee under his wings, yea, so gently sus-
      taineth:
      Hast thou not seen?
      All that is needful hath been
  Granted in what he ordaineth.

3 Praise to the Lord, who doth prosper thy work and
      defend thee;
  Surely his goodness and mercy here daily attend
      thee:
      Ponder anew
      All the Almighty can do,
  He who with love doth befriend thee.

4 Praise to the Lord! O let all that is in me adore him!
  All that hath life and breath come now with praises
        before him!
      Let the amen
      Sound from his people again:
  Gladly for ay we adore him.

14 *Ps.* 148.   *George Wither*, 1588–1667.

THE Lord of Heaven confess;
  On high his glory raise:
Him let all angels bless,
  Him all his armies praise.
    Him glorify
      Sun, moon, and stars;
      Ye higher spheres,
    And cloudy sky.

2 Praise God from earth below,
  Ye dragons, and ye deeps,
Fire, hail, clouds, wind, and snow,
  Whom in command he keeps.
    Praise ye his name,
      Hills great and small,
      Trees low and tall,
    Beasts wild and tame.

3 O let God's name be praised
  Above both earth and sky;
For he his saints hath raised,
  And set their horn on high;
    Yea, they that are
      Of Israel's race,
      Are in his grace
    And ever dear.

15   *F. W. Faber*, 1814–63.

THERE'S a wideness in God's mercy,
  Like the wideness of the sea;
There's a kindness in his justice,
  Which is more than liberty.

There is no place where earth's sorrows
　　Are more felt than up in heaven;
There is no place where earth's failings
　　Have such kindly judgement given.

2 There is grace enough for thousands
　　Of new worlds as great as this;
There is room for fresh creations
　　In that upper home of bliss.
For the love of God is broader
　　Than the measures of man's mind;
And the heart of the Eternal
　　Is most wonderfully kind.

3 But we make his love too narrow
　　By false limits of our own;
And we magnify his strictness
　　With a zeal he will not own.
If our love were but more simple,
　　We should take him at his word;
And our lives would all be sunshine
　　In the sweetness of our Lord.

St. Francis of Assisi, 1182–1226,
tr. W. H. Draper.

16

ALL creatures of our God and King,
　Lift up your voice and with us sing
　　Alleluia, Alleluia!
Thou burning sun with golden beam,
Thou silver moon with softer gleam,
　　O praise him, O praise him,
　　Alleluia, Alleluia, Alleluia!

2 *Thou rushing wind that art so strong,*
Ye clouds that sail in heaven along,
　　O praise him, Alleluia!
Thou rising morn, in praise rejoice,
Ye lights of evening, find a voice.
　　O praise him, O praise him,
　　Alleluia, Alleluia, Alleluia!

3 *Thou flowing water, pure and clear,*
  Make music for thy Lord to hear,
    Alleluia, Alleluia!
  Thou fire so masterful and bright,
  That givest man both warmth and light,
      O praise him, O praise him,
      Alleluia, Alleluia, Alleluia!

4 *Dear mother earth, who day by day*
  Unfoldest blessings on our way,
      O praise him, Alleluia!
  The flowers and fruits that in thee grow,
  Let them his glory also show.
      O praise him, O praise him,
      Alleluia, Alleluia, Alleluia!

5 Let all things their Creator bless,
  And worship him in humbleness,
      O praise him, Alleluia!
  Praise, praise the Father, praise the Son,
  And praise the Spirit, Three in One.
      O praise him, O praise him,
      Alleluia, Alleluia, Alleluia! Amen.

17   *Mrs. C. F. Alexander,‡ 1818-95.*

*A*LL *things bright and beautiful,*
  All creatures great and small,
All things wise and wonderful,
  The Lord God made them all.

2 Each little flower that opens,
    Each little bird that sings,
  He made their glowing colours,
    He made their tiny wings:

3 The purple-headed mountain,
    The river running by,
  The sunset and the morning,
    That brightens up the sky:

4 The cold wind in the winter,
   The pleasant summer sun,
The ripe fruits in the garden,—
   He made them every one:

5 The tall trees in the greenwood,
   The meadows for our play,
The rushes by the water,
   To gather every day:

6 He gave us eyes to see them,
   And lips that we might tell
How great is God Almighty,
   Who has made all things well:

18   *Edward J. Brailsford, 1841–1921.*

ALL things which live below the sky,
   Or move within the sea,
Are creatures of the Lord most high,
   And brothers unto me.

2 I love to hear the robin sing,
   Perched on the highest bough;
To see the rook with purple wing
   Follow the shining plough.

3 I love to watch the swallow skim
   The river in his flight;
To mark, when day is growing dim,
   The glow-worm's silvery light;

4 The sea-gull whiter than the foam,
   The fish that dart beneath;
The lowing cattle coming home;
   The goats upon the heath.

*5 God taught the wren to build her nest,
   The lark to soar above,
The hen to gather to her breast
   The offspring of her love.

*6 Beneath his heaven there's room for all;
    He gives to all their meat;
He sees the meanest sparrow fall
    Unnoticed in the street.

7 Almighty Father, King of Kings,
    The lover of the meek,
Make me a friend of helpless things,
    Defender of the weak.

19 *Johann W. Hey* (1837). *Songs of Praise version.*

CAN you count the stars that brightly
    Twinkle in the midnight sky?
Can you count the clouds, so lightly
    O'er the meadows floating by?
God, the Lord, doth mark their number
With his eyes that never slumber;
    He hath made them, He hath made them,
    He hath made them, every one.

2 Do you know how many children
    Rise each morning blithe and gay?
Can you count their jolly voices,
    Singing sweetly day by day?
God hears all the happy voices,
In their pretty songs rejoices;
    And he loves them, And he loves them
    And he loves them, every one.

20
                    P. Dearmer, 1867–1936.

GOD is love: his the care,
    Tending each, everywhere.
God is love—all is there!
    Jesus came to show him,
    That mankind might know him:
    Sing aloud, loud, loud!
    Sing aloud, loud, loud!
        God is good!
    God is truth! God is beauty! Praise him!

2 None can see God above;
  All have here man to love;
  Thus may we Godward move,
      Finding him in others,
      Holding all men brothers:

3 Jesus lived here for men,
  Strove and died, rose again,
  Rules our hearts, now as then;
      For he came to save us
      By the truth he gave us:

*4 To our Lord praise we sing—
  Light and life, friend and king,
  Coming down love to bring,
      Pattern for our duty,
      Showing God in beauty:

21

Sarah Betts Rhodes, c. 1830–*c.* 1890.

GOD who made the earth,
  The air, the sky, the sea,
Who gave the light its birth,
    Careth for me.

2 God, who made the grass,
    The flower, the fruit, the tree,
  The day and night to pass,
    Careth for me.

3 God who made the sun,
    The moon, the stars, is he
  Who, when life's clouds come on,
    Careth for me.

22

G. W. Briggs, 1875–1959.

I LOVE God's tiny creatures
    That wander wild and free,
The coral-coated lady-bird,
    The velvet humming-bee;
Shy little flowers in hedge and dyke
    That hide themselves away:
God paints them, though they are so small,
    God makes them bright and gay.

2 Dear Father, who hast all things made,
  And carest for them all,
There's none too great for thy great love,
  Nor anything too small:
If thou canst spend such tender care
  On things that grow so wild,
How wonderful thy love must be
  For me, thy loving child.

23   *M. Rinkart, 1586–1649. Tr. C. Winkworth.*

NOW thank we all our God,
    With heart and hands and voices,
Who wondrous things hath done,
  In whom his world rejoices;
Who from our mother's arms
    Hath blessed us on our way
With countless gifts of love,
    And still is ours to-day.

2   O may this bounteous God
  Through all our life be near us,
With ever joyful hearts
  And blessèd peace to cheer us;
And keep us in his grace,
    And guide us when perplexed,
And free us from all ills
    In this world and the next.

3   All praise and thanks to God
  The Father now be given,
The Son, and him who reigns
  With them in highest heaven,
The one eternal God,
    Whom earth and heaven adore;
For thus it was, is now,
    And shall be evermore. Amen.

24 *Ps. 90.*   *I. Watts, 1674–1748.*

O GOD, our help in ages past,
    Our hope for years to come,
Our shelter from the stormy blast,
    And our eternal home;

2 Under the shadow of thy throne
   Thy saints have dwelt secure;
Sufficient is thine arm alone,
   And our defence is sure.

3 Before the hills in order stood,
   Or earth received her frame,
From everlasting thou art God,
   To endless years the same.

4 A thousand ages in thy sight
   Are like an evening gone,
Short as the watch that ends the night
   Before the rising sun.

5 Time, like an ever-rolling stream,
   Bears all its sons away;
They fly forgotten, as a dream
   Dies at the opening day.

6 O God, our help in ages past,
   Our hope for years to come,
Be thou our guard while troubles last,
   And our eternal home.

25   *Ps.* 103.   *H. F. Lyte,* 1793–1847.

PRAISE, my soul, the King of heaven;
   To his feet thy tribute bring.
Ransomed, healed, restored, forgiven,
   Who like me his praise should sing?
     Praise him! Praise him!
   Praise the everlasting King.

2 Praise him for his grace and favour
   To our fathers in distress;
Praise him still the same for ever,
   Slow to chide, and swift to bless.
     Praise him! Praise him!
   Glorious in his faithfulness.

3 Father-like, he tends and spares us;
  Well our feeble frame he knows;
In his hands he gently bears us,
  Rescues us from all our foes.
    Praise him! Praise him!
  Widely as his mercy flows.

4 Angels, help us to adore him;
  Ye behold him face to face;
Sun and moon, bow down before him;
  Dwellers all in time and space.
    Praise him! Praise him!
  Praise with us the God of grace.

26 *Ps. 23.*   *George Herbert, 1593–1632.*

THE God of love my Shepherd is,
  And he that doth me feed;
While he is mine and I am his,
  What can I want or need?

2 He leads me to the tender grass,
  Where I both feed and rest;
Then to the streams that gently pass:
  In both I have the best.

3 Or if I stray, he doth convert,
  And bring my mind in frame,
And all this not for my desert,
  But for his holy name.

4 Yea, in death's shady black abode
  Well may I walk, not fear;
For thou art with me, and thy rod
  To guide, thy staff to bear.

5 Surely thy sweet and wondrous love
  Shall measure all my days;
And as it never shall remove
  So neither shall my praise.

27   *J. Keble, 1792–1866.*

THERE is a book who runs may read,
    Which heavenly truth imparts,
And all the lore its scholars need,
    Pure eyes and Christian hearts.

2 The works of God above, below,
    Within us and around,
Are pages in that book, to show
    How God himself is found.

3 The glorious sky, embracing all,
    Is like the Maker's love,
Wherewith encompassed, great and small
    In peace and order move.

4 The moon above, the Church below,
    A wondrous race they run;
But all their radiance, all their glow,
    Each borrows of its sun.

5 The raging fire, the roaring wind,
    Thy boundless power display;
But in the gentler breeze we find
    Thy Spirit's viewless way.

6 Two worlds are ours: 'tis only sin
    Forbids us to descry
The mystic heaven and earth within,
    Plain as the sea and sky.

7 Thou, who hast given me eyes to see
    And love this sight so fair,
Give me a heart to find out thee,
    And read thee everywhere.

28 *Ps. 23.*   *Sir H. W. Baker, 1821–77.*

THE King of love my Shepherd is,
    Whose goodness faileth never;
I nothing lack if I am his
    And he is mine for ever.

2 Where streams of living water flow
    My ransomed soul he leadeth,
And where the verdant pastures grow
    With food celestial feedeth.

3 Perverse and foolish oft I strayed,
    But yet in love he sought me,
And on his shoulder gently laid,
    And home, rejoicing, brought me.

4 In death's dark vale I fear no ill
    With thee, dear Lord, beside me;
Thy rod and staff my comfort still,
    Thy Cross before to guide me.

5 Thou spread'st a table in my sight;
    Thy unction grace bestoweth:
And O what transport of delight
    From thy pure chalice floweth!

6 And so through all the length of days
    Thy goodness faileth never;
Good Shepherd, may I sing thy praise
    Within thy house for ever.

JESUS CHRIST OUR LORD

29

E. Perronet, 1726–92; and others.

ALL hail the power of Jesus' name;
    Let angels prostrate fall;
Bring forth the royal diadem
    To crown him Lord of all.

2 Crown him, ye martyrs of your God,
    Who from his altar call;
Praise him whose way of pain ye trod,
    And crown him Lord of all.

3 Sinners, whose love can ne'er forget
    The wormwood and the gall,
Go spread your trophies at his feet,
    And crown him Lord of all.

4 Let every tribe and every tongue
　　To him their hearts enthral,
Lift high the universal song,
　　And crown him Lord of all.

30   *G. W. Briggs, 1875-1959.*

CHRIST is the world's true Light,
　　Its Captain of salvation,
The Day-star clear and bright
　　Of every man and nation;
New life, new hope awakes,
　　Where'er men own his sway:
Freedom her bondage breaks,
　　And night is turned to day.

2 In Christ all races meet,
　　Their ancient feuds forgetting,
The whole round world complete,
　　From sunrise to its setting:
When Christ is throned as Lord,
　　Men shall forsake their fear,
To ploughshare beat the sword,
　　To pruning-hook the spear.

3 One Lord, in one great name
　　Unite us all who own thee;
Cast out our pride and shame
　　That hinder to enthrone thee;
The world has waited long,
　　Has travailed long in pain,
To heal its ancient wrong,
　　Come, Prince of Peace, and reign.

31   *I. Watts, 1674-1748.*

COME, let us join our cheerful songs
　　With angels round the throne;
Ten thousand thousand are their tongues,
　　But all their joys are one.

2 'Worthy the Lamb that died', they cry,
    'To be exalted thus';
  'Worthy the Lamb', our lips reply,
    'For he was slain for us.'

3 Jesus is worthy to receive
    Honour and power divine;
  And blessings more than we can give
    Be, Lord, for ever thine.

4 The whole creation join in one
    To bless the sacred name
  Of him that sits upon the throne,
    And to adore the Lamb.

32

J. Newton, 1725–1807.

HOW sweet the name of Jesus sounds
    In a believer's ear!
It soothes his sorrows, heals his wounds,
    And drives away his fear.

2 It makes the wounded spirit whole,
    And calms the troubled breast;
'Tis manna to the hungry soul,
    And to the weary rest.

3 Dear name! the rock on which I build,
    My shield and hiding-place,
My never-failing treasury filled
    With boundless stores of grace.

4 Jesus! my Shepherd, Husband, Friend,
    My Prophet, Priest, and King,
My Lord, my Life, my Way, my End,
    Accept the praise I bring.

5 Weak is the effort of my heart
    And cold my warmest thought;
But when I see thee as thou art,
    I'll praise thee as I ought.

6 Till then I would thy love proclaim
    With every fleeting breath;
And may the music of thy name
    Refresh my soul in death.

33

Stopford A. Brooke, 1832–1916.

IT fell upon a summer day,
  When Jesus walked in Galilee,
The mothers from a village brought
    Their children to his knee.

2 He took them in his arms, and laid
    His hands on each remembered head;
'Suffer these little ones to come
    To me,' he gently said.

3 'Forbid them not; unless ye bear
    The childlike heart your hearts within,
Unto my Kingdom ye may come,
    But may not enter in.'

4 Master, I fain would enter there;
    O let me follow thee, and share
Thy meek and lowly heart, and be
    Freed from all worldly care.

5 Of innocence, and love, and trust,
Of quiet work, and simple word,
Of joy, and thoughtlessness of self,
    Build up my life, good Lord.

34

C. Wesley, 1707–88.

JESU, Lover of my soul,
  Let me to thy bosom fly,
While the nearer waters roll,
  While the tempest still is high:
Hide me, O my Saviour, hide,
  Till the storm of life is past;
Safe into the haven guide,
  O receive my soul at last.

2 Other refuge have I none;
    Hangs my helpless soul on thee;
Leave, ah! leave me not alone,
    Still support and comfort me.
All my trust on thee is stayed,
    All my help from thee I bring;
Cover my defenceless head
    With the shadow of thy wing.

3 Plenteous grace with thee is found,
    Grace to cover all my sin;
Let the healing streams abound;
    Make and keep me pure within.
Thou of life the fountain art;
    Freely let me take of thee;
Spring thou up within my heart,
    Rise to all eternity.

35
*From the Joyful Rhythm of St.
Bernard* (1091–1153). *Tr. E. Caswall.*

JESU, the very thought of thee
    With sweetness fills my breast;
But sweeter far thy face to see,
    And in thy presence rest.

2 Nor voice can sing, nor heart can frame,
    Nor can the memory find,
A sweeter sound than thy blest name,
    O Saviour of mankind!

3 O hope of every contrite heart,
    O joy of all the meek,
To those who fall, how kind thou art!
    How good to those who seek!

4 But what to those who find? Ah! this
    Nor tongue nor pen can show;
The love of Jesus! what it is
    None but his loved ones know.

5 Jesu, our only joy be thou,
    As thou our prize wilt be;
Jesu, be thou our glory now,
    And through eternity.

36
St. Theoctistus, c. 890. *Tr. J. M. Neale.*‡

JESUS, name all names above;
    Jesus, best and dearest;
Jesus, fount of perfect love,
    Holiest, tenderest, nearest;

Thou the source of grace completest;
Thou the purest, thou the sweetest;
Thou the well of power divine,
Make me, keep me, seal me thine!

2 Jesus, crowned with bitter thorn,
 By mankind forsaken,
Jesus, who through scourge and scorn
 Held thy faith unshaken,
Jesus, clad in purple raiment,
For man's evils making payment:
Let not all thy woe and pain,
Let not Calvary be in vain!

37   *P. Dearmer*, 1867–1936.

O DEAR and lovely Brother,
 The Son of God alone,
When we love one another
 We are thy very own.

2 In heaven thy face is hidden
 Too near for us to see;
And each of us is bidden
 To share that heaven with thee.

38   *Charles Wesley*, 1707–88.

O FOR a thousand tongues to sing
 My dear Redeemer's praise,
The glories of my God and King,
 The triumphs of his grace!

2 Jesus—the name that charms our fears,
 That bids our sorrows cease;
'Tis music in the sinner's ears,
 'Tis life, and health, and peace.

3 He speaks;—and, listening to his voice,
 New life the dead receive,
The mournful broken hearts rejoice,
 The humble poor believe.

4 Hear him, ye deaf; his praise, ye dumb,
   Your loosened tongues employ;
Ye blind, behold your Saviour come;
   And leap, ye lame, for joy!

5 My gracious Master and my God,
   Assist me to proclaim
And spread through all the earth abroad
   The honours of thy name.

39
                   J. E. Bode, 1816–74.

O JESUS, I have promised
   To serve thee to the end;
Be thou for ever near me,
   My Master and my Friend;
I shall not fear the battle
   If thou art by my side,
Nor wander from the pathway
   If thou wilt be my guide.

2 O let me feel thee near me:
   The world is ever near;
I see the sights that dazzle,
   The tempting sounds I hear;
My foes are ever near me,
   Around me and within;
But, Jesus, draw thou nearer,
   And shield my soul from sin.

3 O let me hear thee speaking
   In accents clear and still,
Above the storms of passion,
   The murmurs of self-will;
O speak to reassure me,
   To hasten or control;
O speak, and make me listen,
   Thou guardian of my soul.

4 O Jesus, thou hast promised
   To all who follow thee,
That where thou art in glory
   There shall thy servant be;

And, Jesus, I have promised
  To serve thee to the end;
O give me grace to follow,
  My Master and my Friend.

5 O let me see thy footmarks,
  And in them plant mine own;
My hope to follow duly
  Is in thy strength alone;
O guide me, call me, draw me,
  Uphold me to the end;
And then in heaven receive me,
  My Saviour and my Friend.

40   *Frank Fletcher, 1870-1954.*

O SON of man, our hero strong and tender,
  Whose servants are the brave in all the earth,
Our living sacrifice to thee we render,
  Who sharest all our sorrow, all our mirth.

2 O feet so strong to climb the path of duty,
  O lips divine that taught the words of truth,
Kind eyes that marked the lilies in their beauty,
  And heart that kindled at the zeal of youth.

3 Lover of children, boyhood's inspiration,
  Of all mankind the Servant and the King,
O Lord of joy and hope and consolation,
  To thee our fears and joys and hopes we bring.

4 Not in our failures only and our sadness,
  We seek thy presence, Comforter and Friend;
O rich man's guest, be with us in our gladness!
  O poor man's mate, our lowliest tasks attend!

41   *Mrs. C. F. Alexander, 1818-95.*

ONCE in royal David's city
  Stood a lowly cattle shed,
Where a mother laid her baby
  In a manger for his bed;
Mary was that mother mild,
Jesus Christ her little Child.

2 He came down to earth from heaven,
   Who is God and Lord of all,
And his shelter was a stable,
   And his cradle was a stall;
With the poor, and mean, and lowly,
Lived on earth our Saviour holy.

3 And through all his wondrous childhood
   He would honour and obey,
Love, and watch the lowly maiden,
   In whose gentle arms he lay;
Christian children all must be
Mild, obedient, good as he.

4 For he is our childhood's pattern,
   Day by day like us he grew,
He was little, weak, and helpless,
   Tears and smiles like us he knew;
And he feeleth for our sadness,
And he shareth in our gladness.

5 And our eyes at last shall see him,
   Through his own redeeming love,
For that child so dear and gentle
   Is our Lord in heaven above;
And he leads his children on
To the place where he is gone.

42   *William Canton, 1845–1926.*

WHEN the herds were watching
   In the midnight chill,
Came a spotless lambkin
   From the heavenly hill.

2 Snow was on the mountains
   And the wind was cold,
When from God's own garden
   Dropped a rose of gold.

3 When 'twas bitter winter,
   Homeless and forlorn
In a star-lit stable
   Christ the babe was born.

4 Welcome, heavenly lambkin;
  Welcome, golden rose;
Alleluya, baby
  In the swaddling clothes!

43   P. Dearmer, 1867–1936.

WHO within that stable cries,
  Gentle babe that in manger lies?
    'Tis the Lord, our heart replies.
So follow him, his bidding do for ever:
  Together now triumphantly cry,
    Triumphantly cry, with one accord.
  We will praise and glorify
    The Christ, the Lord!
      Ever, ever,
    Jesus, beacon for our high endeavour!

2 Who is he, the man full-grown,
  Working on in the busy town?
    'Tis the Lord, obscure, unknown.
So follow him, his bidding do for ever:

3 Healing lame and blind and dumb,
  Herald now that the Kingdom's come?
    'Tis the friend of every home.
So follow him, his bidding do for ever:

PART II

4 Who is he whom crowds acclaim
  As he enters Jerusalem?
    'Tis the Lord of happy fame.
So follow him, his bidding do for ever:

5 Taken in Gethsemane,
  Martyred on the forlorn cross-tree?
    He who died for you and me.
So follow him, his bidding do for ever:

6 From the tomb triumphant now,
  Deathless splendour upon his brow?
    He to whom all creatures bow.
So follow him, his bidding do for ever:

Conclusion, for either Part

7 Passing still to every place,
   Radiant friend of the human race!
      'Tis the Lord, the fount of grace.
   So follow him, his bidding do for ever:
(*The verses may be sung as a solo, the refrain being sung by all.*)

HIS ADVENT

44

P. Doddridge, 1702–51.

HARK the glad sound! the Saviour comes,
  The Saviour promised long!
Let every heart prepare a throne,
  And every voice a song.

2 He comes the prisoners to release
  In Satan's bondage held;
The gates of brass before him burst,
  The iron fetters yield.

3 He comes the broken heart to bind,
  The bleeding soul to cure,
And with the treasures of his grace
  To enrich the humble poor.

4 Our glad hosannas, Prince of peace,
  Thy welcome shall proclaim;
And heaven's eternal arches ring
  With thy belovèd name.

45

18th cent. Tr. T. A. Lacey.

O COME, O come, Emmanuel!
  Redeem thy captive Israel,
That into exile drear is gone
Far from the face of God's dear Son:
  Rejoice! Rejoice! Emmanuel
  Shall come to thee, O Israel.

2 O come, O come, thou Dayspring bright!
Pour on our souls thy healing light;
Dispel the long night's lingering gloom,
And pierce the shadows of the tomb:

3 O come, thou Lord of David's key!
  The royal door fling wide and free;
  Safeguard for us the heavenward road,
  And bar the way to death's abode:

4 O come, O come, Adonaï,
  Who in thy glorious majesty
  From that high mountain clothed with awe
  Gavest thy folk the elder law:

(For Advent see also The Spread of the Kingdom, Hymns 134-143.)

HIS BIRTH

46   *John Byrom,† 1692-1763.*

CHRISTIANS, awake, salute the happy morn,
  Whereon the Saviour of the world was born;
Rise to adore the mystery of love,
Which hosts of Angels chanted from above;
With them the joyful tidings first begun
Of God incarnate and the Virgin's Son:

2 Then to the watchful shepherds it was told,
  Who heard the angelic herald's voice, 'Behold,
  I bring good tidings of a Saviour's birth
  To you and all the nations upon earth;
  This day hath God fulfilled his promised word,
  This day is born a Saviour, Christ the Lord.'

3 He spake; and straightway the celestial choir
  In hymns of joy, unknown before, conspire.
  The praises of redeeming love they sang,
  And heaven's whole orb with Alleluyas rang:
  God's highest glory was their anthem still,
  Peace upon earth, and unto men good will.

*4 To Bethlehem straight the enlightened shepherds
    ran,
  To see the wonder God had wrought for man.
  He that was born upon this joyful day
  Around us all his glory shall display:
  Saved by his love, incessant we shall sing
  Eternal praise to heaven's almighty King.

47   *Nahum Tate, 1652–1715.*

WHILE shepherds watched their flocks by night,
    All seated on the ground,
The Angel of the Lord came down,
    And glory shone around.

2 'Fear not,' said he (for mighty dread
    Had seized their troubled mind);
'Glad tidings of great joy I bring
    To you and all mankind.

3 'To you in David's town this day
    Is born of David's line
A Saviour, who is Christ the Lord;
    And this shall be the sign:

4 'The heavenly Babe you there shall find
    To human view displayed,
All meanly wrapped in swathing bands,
    And in a manger laid.'

5 Thus spake the Seraph: and forthwith
    Appeared a shining throng
Of Angels praising God, who thus
    Addressed their joyful song:

6 'All glory be to God on high,
    And to the earth be peace;
Good-will henceforth from heaven to men
    Begin and never cease.'

48   *C. Wesley* (1743), *G. Whitefield* (1753),
             M. Madan (1760), *and others.*

HARK! the herald Angels sing
    Glory to the new-born King;
Peace on earth and mercy mild,
God and sinners reconciled:
Joyful all ye nations rise,
Join the triumph of the skies,
With the angelic host proclaim,
Christ is born in Bethlehem:
       Hark! the herald Angels sing
       Glory to the new-born King.

2 Christ, by highest heaven adored,
  Christ, the everlasting Lord,
Late in time behold him come
Offspring of the Virgin's womb!
  Veiled in flesh the Godhead see,
  Hail the incarnate Deity!
  Pleased as man with man to dwell,
  Jesus, our Emmanuel:

3 Hail the heaven-born Prince of peace!
  Hail the Sun of Righteousness!
Light and life to all he brings,
Risen with healing in his wings;
  Mild he lays his glory by,
  Born that man no more may die,
  Born to raise the sons of earth,
  Born to give them second birth:
        Hark! the herald Angels sing
        Glory to the new-born King.

49   18th *cent. Tr. F. Oakeley, and others.*

O COME, all ye faithful,
    Joyful and triumphant,
O come ye, O come ye to Bethlehem;
  Come and behold him,
  Born the King of Angels:
      O come, let us adore him,
      O come, let us adore him,
      O come, let us adore him, Christ the Lord!

*2 See how the Shepherds,
      Summoned to his cradle,
  Leaving their flocks, draw nigh to gaze;
    We too will thither
    Bend our joyful footsteps:

*3 Lo! star-led chieftains,
      Magi, Christ adoring,
  Offer him incense, gold, and myrrh;
    We to the Christ Child
    Bring our hearts' oblations:

4 Child, for us sinners
 Poor and in the manger,
Fain we embrace thee, with love and awe;
 Who would not love thee,
 Loving us so dearly?

5 Sing, choirs of Angels,
 Sing in exultation,
Sing, all ye citizens of heaven above;
 Glory to God
 In the highest:

(Christmas Day only)

6 Yea, Lord, we greet thee,
 Born this happy morning,
Jesu, to thee be glory given;
 Word of the Father,
 Now in flesh appearing:

50 *Bishop Phillips Brooks, 1835–93.*

O LITTLE town of Bethlehem,
 How still we see thee lie!
Above thy deep and dreamless sleep
 The silent stars go by.
Yet in thy dark streets shineth
 The everlasting light;
The hopes and fears of all the years
 Are met in thee to-night.

2 O morning stars, together
 Proclaim the holy birth,
And praises sing to God the King,
 And peace to men on earth;
For Christ is born of Mary;
 And, gathered all above,
While mortals sleep, the angels keep
 Their watch of wondering love.

3 How silently, how silently,
 The wondrous gift is given!
So God imparts to human hearts
 The blessings of his heaven.

No ear may hear his coming;
    But in this world of sin,
Where meek souls will receive him still,
    The dear Christ enters in.

4 Where children pure and happy
    Pray to the blessèd Child,
Where misery cries out to thee,
    Son of the mother mild;
Where charity stands watching
    And faith holds wide the door,
The dark night wakes, the glory breaks,
    And Christmas comes once more.

5 O holy Child of Bethlehem,
    Descend to us, we pray;
Cast out our sin, and enter in,
    Be born in us to-day.
We hear the Christmas Angels
    The great glad tidings tell:
O come to us, abide with us,
    Our Lord Emmanuel.

51
Laurence Housman, 1865–1959.

WHEN Christ was born in Bethlehem,
    Fair peace on earth to bring,
In lowly state of love he came
    To be the children's King.

2 A mother's heart was there his throne,
    His orb a maiden's breast,
Whereby he made through love alone
    His kingdom manifest.

3 And round him, then, a holy band
    Of children blest was born,
Fair guardians of his throne to stand
    Attendant night and morn.

4 And unto them this grace was given
    A Saviour's name to own,
And die for him who out of heaven
    Had found on earth a throne.

5 O blessèd babes of Bethlehem,
    Who died to save our King,
Ye share the martyrs' diadem,
    And in their anthem sing!

6 Your lips, on earth that never spake,
    Now sound the eternal word;
And in the courts of love ye make
    Your children's voices heard.

7 Lord Jesus Christ, eternal Child,
    Make thou our childhood thine;
That we with thee the meek and mild
    May share the love divine.

HIS EPIPHANY

52

W. Chatterton Dix, 1837–98.

As with gladness men of old
    Did the guiding star behold,
As with joy they hailed its light,
Leading onward, beaming bright,
    So, most gracious God, may we
    Evermore be led to thee.

2 As with joyful steps they sped,
    To that lowly manger-bed,
There to bend the knee before
Him whom heaven and earth adore,
    So may we with willing feet
    Ever seek thy mercy-seat.

3 As they offered gifts most rare
    At that manger rude and bare,
So may we with holy joy,
Pure, and free from sin's alloy,
    All our costliest treasures bring,
    Christ, to thee our heavenly King.

4 Holy Jesu, every day
  Keep us in the narrow way;
And, when earthly things are past,
Bring our ransomed souls at last
Where they need no star to guide,
Where no clouds thy glory hide.

5 In the heavenly country bright
  Need they no created light;
Thou its light, its joy, its crown,
Thou its sun which goes not down:
There for ever may we sing
Alleluyas to our King.

53   *Prudentius, 348–c. 413. Tr. E. Caswall.*

BETHLEHEM, of noblest cities
  None can once with thee compare;
Thou alone the Lord from heaven
  Didst for us incarnate bear.

2 Fairer than the sun at morning
  Was the star that told his birth;
To the lands their God announcing,
  Hid beneath a form of earth.

3 By its lambent beauty guided
  See the eastern kings appear;
See them bend, their gifts to offer,
  Gifts of incense, gold and myrrh.

4 Solemn things of mystic meaning:
  Incense doth the God disclose,
Gold a royal child proclaimeth,
  Myrrh a future tomb foreshows.

5 Holy Jesu, in thy brightness
  To the Gentile world displayed
With the Father and the Spirit
  Endless praise to thee be paid.

(For Epiphany see also The Spread of the Kingdom,
Hymns 134–143.)

THE PRESENTATION IN THE TEMPLE

54 *Jan Struther, 1901–53.*

WHEN Mary brought her treasure
　Unto the holy place,
No eye of man could measure
　The joy upon her face.
　　He was but six weeks old,
Her plaything and her pleasure,
　Her silver and her gold.

2 Then Simeon, on him gazing
　With wonder and with love,
His aged voice up-raising
　Gave thanks to God above:
　　'Now welcome sweet release!
For I, my saviour praising,
　May die at last in peace.'

3 And she, all sorrow scorning,
　Rejoiced in Jesus' fame.
The child her arms adorning
　Shone softly like a flame
　　That burns the long night through,
And keeps from dusk till morning
　Its vigil clear and true.

4 As by the sun in splendour
　The flags of night are furled,
So darkness shall surrender
　To Christ who lights the world:
　　To Christ the star of day,
Who once was small and tender,
　A candle's gentle ray.

HIS TEMPTATION IN THE WILDERNESS

55 *G. H. Smyttan, 1825–70, and others.*

FORTY days and forty nights
　Thou wast fasting in the wild;
Forty days and forty nights
　Tempted still, yet unbeguiled:

2 Sunbeams scorching all the day,
  Chilly dew-drops nightly shed,
  Prowling beasts about thy way,
  Stones thy pillow, earth thy bed.

3 Let us thy endurance share
  And from earthly greed abstain,
  With thee watching unto prayer,
  With thee strong to suffer pain.

*4 Then if evil on us press,
  Flesh or spirit to assail,
  Victor in the wilderness,
  Help us not to swerve or fail!

5 So shall peace divine be ours;
  Holier gladness ours shall be;
  Come to us angelic powers,
  Such as ministered to thee.

6 Keep, O keep us, Saviour dear,
  Ever constant by thy side,
  That with thee we may appear
  At the eternal Eastertide.

(*For Lent hymns see also The Way of Life* 68–87, *and Prayer*
123–133.
For our Lord's ministry see 33, 40, 43, 71, 79, 83.)

HIS PATHWAY TO THE CROSS

56

St. Theodulph of Orleans, d. 821.
Tr. J. M. Neale.

*A*LL glory, laud, and honour
  To thee, Redeemer, King,
To whom the lips of children
  Made sweet hosannas ring.

2 Thou art the King of Israel,
  Thou David's royal Son,
  Who in the Lord's name comest,
  The King and blessèd one:

3 The company of Angels
   Are praising thee on high,
And mortal men and all things
   Created make reply:

4 The people of the Hebrews
   With palms before thee went;
Our praise and prayer and anthems
   Before thee we present:

5 To thee before thy passion
   They sang their hymns of praise;
To thee now high exalted
   Our melody we raise:

6 Thou didst accept their praises,
   Accept the prayers we bring,
Who in all good delightest,
   Thou good and gracious King:

57   *G. Moultrie, 1829–85.*

COME, faithful people, come away,
   Your homage to your Monarch pay;
It is the feast of palms to-day:
   Hosanna in the highest!

2 When Christ, the Lord of all, drew nigh
On Sunday morn to Bethany,
He called two loved ones standing by:

3 'To yonder village go,' said he,
'Where you a tethered ass shall see;
Loose it and bring it unto me':

4 The two upon their errand sped,
And brought the ass as he had said,
And on its back their clothes they spread:

5 They set him on his throne so rude;
Before him went the multitude,
And in the way their garments strewed:

*6 Go, Saviour, thus to triumph borne,
Thy crown shall be the wreath of thorn,
Thy royal garb the robe of scorn:

*7 They thronged before, behind, around,
They cast palm-branches on the ground,
And still rose up the joyful sound:

*8 'Blessèd is Israel's King,' they cry;
'Blessèd is he that cometh nigh
In name of God the Lord most High':

9 Thus, Saviour, to thy Passion go;
Pass through the fleeting ebb and flow,
To meet the yet unconquered foe:
    Hosanna in the highest!

58   *H. H. Milman,* 1791–1868.

RIDE on! ride on in majesty!
    Hark, all the tribes hosanna cry;
Thine humble beast pursues his road
With palms and scattered garments strowed.

2 Ride on! ride on in majesty!
In lowly pomp ride on to die:
O Christ, thy triumphs now begin
O'er captive death and conquered sin.

3 Ride on! ride on in majesty!
The wingèd squadrons of the sky
Look down with sad and wondering eyes
To see the approaching sacrifice.

4 Ride on! ride on in majesty!
Thy last and fiercest strife is nigh;
The Father, on his sapphire throne,
Expects his own anointed Son.

5 Ride on! ride on in majesty!
In lowly pomp ride on to die;
Bow thy meek head to mortal pain,
Then take, O God, thy power, and reign.

HIS CROSS AND PASSION

59

Mrs. C. F. Alexander, 1818-95.

THERE is a green hill far away,
　Without a city wall,
Where the dear Lord was crucified
　Who died to save us all.

2 We may not know, we cannot tell,
　What pains he had to bear
But we believe it was for us
　He hung and suffered there.

3 He died that we might be forgiven,
　He died to make us good;
That we might go at last to heaven,
　Saved by his precious blood.

4 O, dearly, dearly has he loved,
　And we must love him too,
And trust in his redeeming Blood,
　And try his works to do.

60

I. Watts, 1674-1748.

WHEN I survey the wondrous Cross,
　On which the Prince of glory died,
My richest gain I count but loss,
　And pour contempt on all my pride.

2 Forbid it, Lord, that I should boast
　Save in the death of Christ my God;
All the vain things that charm me most,
　I sacrifice them to his blood.

3 See from his head, his hands, his feet,
　Sorrow and love flow mingled down;
Did e'er such love and sorrow meet,
　Or thorns compose so rich a crown?

4 Were the whole realm of nature mine,
　That were a present far too small;
Love so amazing, so divine,
　Demands my soul, my life, my all.

HIS RESURRECTION

61

Lyra Davidica (1708), and the Supplement (1816).
Based partly on Surrexit Christus hodie, c. 14th cent.

JESUS Christ is risen to-day,
　　　　　Alleluya!
Out triumphant holy day,
　　　　　Alleluya!
Who did once, upon the Cross,
　　　　　Alleluya!
Suffer to redeem our loss.
　　　　　Alleluya!

2 Hymns of praise then let us sing,
Unto Christ, our heavenly King,
Who endured the Cross and grave,
Sinners to redeem and save!

3 But the pains that he endured
Our salvation have procured;
Now above the sky he's King,
Where the angels ever sing:
　　　　　Alleluya!

62　　　　　*Ascribed to 17th cent. Tr. J. M. Neale.‡*

ALLELUYA! Alleluya! Alleluya!
Ye sons and daughters of the King,
Whom heavenly hosts in glory sing,
To-day the grave hath lost its sting:
　　　　　Alleluya!

2 On that first morning of the week,
Before the day began to break,
The Marys went their Lord to seek:
　　　　　Alleluya!

3 A young man bade their sorrow flee,
For thus he spake unto the three:
'Your Lord is gone to Galilee':
　　　　　Alleluya!

4 That night the Apostles met in fear,
Amidst them came their Lord most dear,
And greeted them with words of cheer:
Alleluya!

5 When Thomas afterwards had heard
That Jesus had fulfilled his word,
He doubted if it were the Lord:
Alleluya!

6 'Thomas, behold my side,' saith he.
'My hands, my feet, my body see;
And doubt not, but believe in me':
Alleluya!

7 No longer Thomas then denied;
He saw the feet, the hands, the side;
'Thou art my Lord and God,' he cried:
Alleluya!

*8 Blessèd are they that have not seen,
And yet whose faith hath constant been,
In life eternal they shall reign:
Alleluya!

63
C. A. Alington, 1872–1955.

GOOD Christian men rejoice and sing!
Now is the triumph of our King!
To all the world glad news we bring:
Alleluya! Alleluya! Alleluya!

2 The Lord of Life is risen for ay;
Bring flowers of song to strew his way;
Let all mankind rejoice and say:

3 Praise we in songs of victory
That Love, that Life which cannot die,
And sing with hearts uplifted high:

4 Thy name we bless, O risen Lord,
And sing to-day with one accord
The life laid down, the Life restored:

64   *Ascribed to 17th cent. Tr. F. Pott.*

THE strife is o'er, the battle done;
 Now is the Victor's triumph won;
O let the song of praise be sung: *Alleluya!*

2 Death's mightiest powers have done their worst,
 And Jesus hath his foes dispersed;
Let shouts of praise and joy outburst: *Alleluya!*

3 On the third morn he rose again
 Glorious in majesty to reign;
O let us swell the joyful strain: *Alleluya!*

4 Lord, by the stripes which wounded thee,
 From death's dread sting thy servants free,
That we may live, and sing to thee: *Alleluya!*

65   *St. John Damascene, c. 750. Tr. J. M. Neale.‡*

COME, ye faithful, raise the strain
 Of triumphant gladness;
God hath brought his people now
 Into joy from sadness;
'Tis the spring of souls to-day;
 Christ hath burst his prison,
And from three days' sleep in death
 As a sun hath risen.

2 Now the queen of seasons, bright
 With the day of splendour,
With the royal feast of feasts,
 Comes its joy to render;
Comes to gladden Christian men,
 Who with true affection
Welcome in unwearied strains
 Jesus' resurrection.

3 Neither might the gates of death,
 Nor the tomb's dark portal,
Nor the wrappings, nor the stone,
 Hold thee as a mortal;
But to-day amidst the twelve
 Thou didst stand, bestowing
Thine own peace which evermore
 Passeth human knowing.

HIS ASCENSION

66   *T. Kelly*, 1769–1854.

THE head that once was crowned with thorns
  Is crowned with glory now:
A royal diadem adorns
  The mighty Victor's brow.

2 The highest place that heaven affords
   Is his, is his by right,
The King of kings and Lord of lords,
   And heaven's eternal Light;

3 The joy of all who dwell above,
   The joy of all below,
To whom he manifests his love,
   And grants his name to know.

4 To them the Cross, with all its shame,
   With all its grace is given:
Their name an everlasting name,
   Their joy the joy of heaven.

5 They suffer with their Lord below,
   They reign with him above,
Their profit and their joy to know
   The mystery of his love.

6 The Cross he bore is life and health,
   Though shame and death to him;
His people's hope, his people's wealth,
   Their everlasting theme.

67   *F. C. Burkitt*, 1864–1935.

OUR Lord, his Passion ended,
  Hath gloriously ascended,
Yet though from him divided,
He leaves us not unguided;
  All his benefits to crown
  He hath sent his Spirit down,
Burning like a flame of fire
His disciples to inspire.

2 God's Spirit is directing,
No more they sit expecting,
But forth to all the nation
They go with exultation;
    That which God in them hath wrought
    Fills their life and soul and thought,
    So their witness now can do
    Work as great in others too.

3 The centuries go gliding,
But still we have abiding
With us that Spirit holy
To make us brave and lowly—
    Lowly, for we feel our need,
    God alone is strong indeed;
    Brave, for with the Spirit's aid
    We can venture unafraid.

(Suitable also for Whitsuntide. See also Hymns 88–93. For Trinity (since the Trinity is also the Unity of God), Hymns 1–14 are suitable: especially 4.)

THE WAY OF LIFE

68   *J. Cennick, 1718–55.*

CHILDREN of the heavenly King,
    As ye journey sweetly sing;
Sing your Saviour's worthy praise,
Glorious in his works and ways.

2 We are travelling home to God
In the way the fathers trod;
They are happy now, and we
Soon their happiness shall see.

3 Fear not, brethren, joyful stand
On the borders of your land;
Jesus Christ your Father's Son
Bids you undismayed go on.

4 Lord, obediently we go,
Gladly leaving all below;
Only thou our Leader be,
And we still will follow thee.

69
J. S. B. Monsell, 1811–75.

FIGHT the good fight with all thy might,
    Christ is thy strength, and Christ thy right;
Lay hold on life, and it shall be
    Thy joy and crown eternally.

2 Run the straight race through God's good grace,
    Lift up thine eyes, and seek his face;
Life with its way before us lies,
    Christ is the path, and Christ the prize.

3 Cast care aside, upon thy Guide
    Lean, and his mercy will provide;
Lean, and the trusting soul shall prove
    Christ is its life, and Christ its love.

4 Faint not nor fear, his arms are near,
    He changeth not, and thou art dear;
Only believe, and thou shalt see
    That Christ is all in all to thee.

70
R. Bridges, 1844–1930, based on O quam juvat.
C. Coffin (1736).

HAPPY are they, they that love God,
    Whose hearts have Christ confest,
Who by his cross have found their life,
    And 'neath his yoke their rest.

2 Glad is the praise, sweet are the songs,
    When they together sing;
And strong the prayers that bow the ear
    Of heaven's eternal King.

3 Christ to their homes giveth his peace,
    And makes their loves his own:
But ah, what tares the evil one
    Hath in his garden sown.

4 Sad were our lot, evil this earth,
    Did not its sorrows prove
The path whereby the sheep may find
    The fold of Jesus' love.

5 Then shall they know, they that love him,
     How all their pain is good;
 And death itself cannot unbind
     Their happy brotherhood.

71   *W. Charter Piggott*, 1872–1943.

HEAVENLY Father, may thy blessing
     Rest upon thy children now,
When in praise thy name they hallow,
     When in prayer to thee they bow:
In the wondrous story reading
     Of the Lord of truth and grace,
May they see thy love reflected
     In the light of his dear face.

2 May they learn from this great story
     All the arts of friendliness;
 Truthful speech and honest action,
     Courage, patience, steadfastness;
 How to master self and temper,
     How to make their conduct fair;
 When to speak and when be silent,
     When to do and when forbear.

3 May his spirit wise and holy
     With his gifts their spirits bless,
 Make them loving, joyous, peaceful,
     Rich in goodness, gentleness,
 Strong in self-control, and faithful,
     Kind in thought and deed; for he
 Sayeth, 'What ye do for others
     Ye are doing unto me.'

72   *Charles Wesley*, 1707–88.

HELP us to help each other, Lord,
     Each other's cross to bear,
 Let each his friendly aid afford
     And feel his brother's care.

2 Up into thee, our living head,
    Let us in all things grow,
Till thou hast made us free indeed,
    And spotless here below.

3 Touched by the loadstone of thy love,
    Let all our hearts agree;
And ever toward each other move,
    And ever move toward thee.

73 *Village Hymn.*   *Norman Gale, 1862–1942.*

HERE in the country's heart
    Where the grass is green,
Life is the same sweet life
    As it e'er hath been.

2 Trust in a God still lives,
    And the bell at morn
Floats with a thought of God
    O'er the rising corn.

3 God comes down in the rain,
    And the crop grows tall—
This is the country faith,
    And the best of all.

74   *P. Dearmer, 1867–1936, after J. Bunyan,*
                                    1628–88.

HE who would valiant be
    'Gainst all disaster,
Let him in constancy
        Follow the Master.
There's no discouragement
Shall make him once relent
His first avowed intent
        To be a pilgrim.

2 Who so beset him round
        With dismal stories,
Do but themselves confound—
        His strength the more is.

No foes shall stay his might,
Though he with giants fight:
He will make good his right
    To be a pilgrim.

3 Since, Lord, thou dost defend
    Us with thy Spirit,
We know we at the end
    Shall life inherit.
Then fancies flee away!
I'll fear not what men say,
I'll labour night and day
    To be a pilgrim.

ORIGINAL VERSION
from Bunyan's *Pilgrim's Progress*

WHO would true valour see,
    Let him come hither;
One here will constant be,
    Come wind, come weather;
There's no discouragement
Shall make him once relent
His first avowed intent
    To be a pilgrim.

2 Whoso beset him round
    With dismal stories,
Do but themselves confound;
    His strength the more is.
No lion can him fright,
He'll with a giant fight,
But he will have a right
    To be a pilgrim.

3 Hobgoblin nor foul fiend
    Can daunt his spirit;
He knows he at the end
    Shall life inherit.
Then fancies fly away;
He'll fear not what men say;
He'll labour night and day
    To be a pilgrim.

75

J. Addison,‡ 1672-1719.

HOW are thy servants blest, O Lord!
　　How sure is their defence!
Eternal Wisdom is their guide,
　　Their help Omnipotence.

2 In foreign realms and lands remote,
　　Supported by thy care,
Through burning climes they pass unhurt,
　　And breathe in tainted air.

3 From all their griefs and dangers, Lord,
　　Thy mercy sets them free,
While in the confidence of prayer
　　Their souls take hold on thee.

4 In midst of dangers, fears, and death,
　　Thy goodness we'll adore;
And praise thee for thy mercies past,
　　And humbly hope for more.

5 Our life, while thou preserv'st that life,
　　Thy sacrifice shall be;
And death, when death shall be our lot,
　　Shall join our souls to thee.

76

Lucy Larcom, 1826-93.

I LEARNED it in the meadow path,
　　I learned it on the mountain stairs,
The best things any mortal hath
　　Are those which every mortal shares.

2 The air we breathe, the sky, the breeze,
　　The light without us and within,
Life with its unlocked treasuries,
　　God's riches are for all to win.

3 The grass is softer to my tread,
　　Because it rests unnumbered feet;
Sweeter to me the wild rose red,
　　Because she makes the whole world sweet.

4 And up the radiant peopled way
　　That opens into worlds unknown
　It will be life's delight to say
　　'Heaven is not heaven for me alone'.

5 Wealth won by other's poverty—
　　Not such be mine! let me be blest
　Only in what they share with me,
　　And what I share with all the rest.

77 *School-days.*　　*W. Charter Piggott, 1872–1943.*

IN our work and in our play,
　　Jesus, be thou ever near;
Guarding, guiding all the day,
　　Keep us in thy presence dear.

2 Thou, who at thy mother's knee
　　Learned to hearken and obey,
　Then, work done, ran happily
　　With the children to their play;

3 And by Joseph's bench did stand,
　　Holding his edged tools, as he
　Guiding them with skilful hand,
　　Made a carpenter of thee;

4 Help us, that with eager mind
　　We may learn both fact and rule,
　Patient, diligent and kind
　　In the comradeship of school.

5 Help us, too, in sport and game
　　Gallantly to play our part;
　Win or lose, to keep the same
　　Dauntless spirit and brave heart.

6 May we grow like him in grace,
　　True in mind and pure of soul,
　Meeting life with steadfast face,
　　Run its race and reach the goal.

78

Mrs. J. A. Carney‡ (1845).

LITTLE drops of water,
    Little grains of sand,
Make the mighty ocean
    And the beauteous land.

2 Little deeds of kindness,
    Little words of love,
Make our earth an Eden,
    Like the heavens above.

3 Little seeds of mercy
    Sown by youthful hands,
Grow to bless the nations
    Far in other lands.

4 Glory then for ever
    Be to God on high,
Beautiful and loving,
    To eternity.

79 *All-Day Hymn.*   *Jan Struther,* 1901–53.

LORD of all hopefulness, Lord of all joy,
    Whose trust, ever childlike, no cares could
    destroy,
Be there at our waking, and give us, we pray,
Your bliss in our hearts, Lord, at the break of the
    day.

2 Lord of all eagerness, Lord of all faith,
    Whose strong hands were skilled at the plane and
    the lathe,
Be there at our labours, and give us, we pray,
Your strength in our hearts, Lord, at the noon of
    the day.

3 Lord of all kindliness, Lord of all grace,
    Your hands swift to welcome, your arms to em-
    brace,
Be there at our homing, and give us, we pray,
Your love in our hearts, Lord, at the eve of the day.

4 Lord of all gentleness, Lord of all calm,
    Whose voice is contentment, whose presence is
        balm,
    Be there at our sleeping, and give us, we pray,
    Your peace in our hearts, Lord, at the end of the
        day.

80   *P. Dearmer*, 1867–1936.

LORD of health, thou life within us,
    Strength of all that lives and grows,
Love that meets our hearts to win us,
    Beauty that around us glows,
    Take the praise that brims and flows!

2 Praise for all our work and leisure,
    Mirth and games and jollity,
Study, science, all the treasure
    That is stored by memory,
    Skill of mind and hand and eye;

3 Praise for joys, for sorrows even,
    All that leads us up to thee;
Most of all that out from heaven
    Came thy Son to set us free,
    Came to show us what to be.

4 May our work be keen and willing;
    Make us true to thee and wise;
Help us now, each moment filling,
    Skill and service be our prize,
    Till to thy far hills we rise.

81   *Sir H. W. Baker*,† 1821–77.

LORD, thy word abideth,
    And our footsteps guideth;
Who its truth believeth
Light and joy receiveth.

2 When our foes are near us,
    Then thy word doth cheer us,
Word of consolation,
Message of salvation.

3 When the storms are o'er us
And dark clouds before us,
Then its light directeth
And our way protecteth.

4 Who can tell the pleasure,
Who recount the treasure,
By thy word imparted
To the simple-hearted?

5 Word of mercy, giving
Succour to the living;
Word of life, supplying
Comfort to the dying.

6 O that we, discerning
Its most holy learning,
Lord, may love and hear thee,
Evermore be near thee!

82 *Truth.* *Ernest Myers*, 1844–1921.

NOW in life's breezy morning
Here on life's sunny shore,
To all the powers of falsehood
We vow eternal war:

2 Eternal hate to falsehood;
And then, as needs must be,
O Truth, O lady peerless,
Eternal love to thee.

3 All fair things that seem true things,
Our hearts shall ay receive,
Not over-quick to seize them,
Nor over-loth to leave;

4 Not over-loth or hasty
To leave them or to seize,
Not eager still to wander
Nor clinging still to ease.

5 But one vow links us ever,
That whatsoe'er shall be,
Nor life nor death shall sever
Our souls, O Truth, from thee.

83

J. M. Neale, 1818–66.

O HAPPY band of pilgrims,
 If onward ye will tread
With Jesus as your fellow
 To Jesus as your Head!

2 O happy if ye labour
 As Jesus did for men;
O happy if ye hunger
 As Jesus hungered then!

3 The trials that beset you,
 The sorrows ye endure,
The manifold temptations
 That death alone can cure,

4 What are they but his jewels
 Of right celestial worth?
What are they but the ladder
 Set up to heaven on earth?

5 O happy band of pilgrims,
 Look upward to the skies,
Where such a light affliction
 Shall win you such a prize!

84

*H. Kirke White (1785–1806),
and others (1827).*

OFT in danger, oft in woe,
 Onward, Christians, onward go;
Bear the toil, maintain the strife,
Strengthened with the Bread of Life.

2 Onward, Christians, onward go,
Join the war, and face the foe;
Will ye flee in danger's hour?
Know ye not your Captain's power?

3 Let your drooping hearts be glad;
March in heavenly armour clad;
Fight, nor think the battle long,
Victory soon shall tune your song.

4 Let not sorrow dim your eye,
　Soon shall every tear be dry;
　Let not fears your course impede,
　Great your strength, if great your need.

5 Onward then in battle move;
　More than conquerors ye shall prove;
　Though opposed by many a foe,
　Christian soldiers, onward go.

85　　　　　　　　　*Charles Wesley, 1707–88.*

SOLDIERS of Christ, arise,
　And put your armour on;
Strong in the strength which God supplies,
　Through his eternal Son;
　Strong in the Lord of Hosts,
　And in his mighty power;
Who in the strength of Jesus trusts
　Is more than conqueror.

2　Stand then in his great might,
　　With all his strength endued;
And take, to arm you for the fight,
　　The panoply of God.
　　To keep your armour bright
　　Attend with constant care,
Still walking in your Captain's sight,
　　And watching unto prayer.

3　From strength to strength go on,
　　Wrestle, and fight, and pray;
Tread all the powers of darkness down,
　　And win the well-fought day.
　　That having all things done,
　　And all your conflicts past,
Ye may o'ercome, through Christ alone,
　　And stand entire at last.

86

Bishop W. W. How, 1823–97.

SOLDIERS of the cross, arise!
  Gird you with your armour bright;
Mighty are your enemies,
  Hard the battle ye must fight.

2 'Mid the homes of want and woe,
  Strangers to the living word,
Let the Saviour's herald go,
  Let the voice of hope be heard.

3 Where the shadows deepest lie,
  Carry truth's unsullied ray;
Where are crimes of blackest dye,
  There the saving sign display.

4 To the weary and the worn
  Tell of realms where sorrows cease;
To the outcast and forlorn
  Speak of mercy and of peace.

*5 Guard the helpless; seek the strayed;
  Comfort troubles; banish grief;
In the might of God arrayed,
  Scatter sin and unbelief.

6 Be the banner still unfurled,
  Still unsheathed the Spirit's sword,
Till the kingdoms of the world
  Are the Kingdom of the Lord.

87

B. S. Ingemann, 1798–1862.
Tr. S. Baring-Gould.

THROUGH the night of doubt and sorrow
  Onward goes the pilgrim band,
Singing songs of expectation,
  Marching to the Promised Land.

2 Clear before us through the darkness
  Gleams and burns the guiding light;
Brother clasps the hand of brother,
  Stepping fearless through the night.

3 One the light of God's own presence
   O'er his ransomed people shed,
   Chasing far the gloom and terror,
   Brightening all the path we tread;

4 One the object of our journey,
   One the faith which never tires,
   One the earnest looking forward,
   One the hope our God inspires:

5 One the strain that lips of thousands
   Lift as from the heart of one;
   One the conflict, one the peril,
   One the march in God begun;

6 One the gladness of rejoicing
   On the far eternal shore,
   Where the One Almighty Father
   Reigns in love for evermore.

7 Onward, therefore, pilgrim brothers,
   Onward with the Cross our aid;
   Bear its shame, and fight its battle,
   Till we rest beneath its shade.

8 Soon shall come the great awaking,
   Soon the rending of the tomb;
   Then the scattering of all shadows,
   And the end of toil and gloom.

THE GUIDANCE OF THE HOLY SPIRIT
88

Edwin Hatch, 1835–89.

BREATHE on me, Breath of God,
   Fill me with life anew,
That I may love what thou dost love,
   And do what thou wouldst do.

2 Breathe on me, Breath of God,
   Until my heart is pure,
   Until with thee I will one will,
   To do and to endure.

3 Breathe on me, Breath of God,
Blend all my soul with thine,
Until this earthly part of me
Glows with the fire divine.

4 Breathe on me, Breath of God,
So shall I never die,
But live with thee the perfect life
Of thine eternity.

89 *The Eternal Spirit.*   *P. Dearmer, 1867–1936.*

O HOLY Spirit, God,
All loveliness is thine;
Great things and small are both in thee,
The star-world is thy shrine.

2 The sunshine thou of God,
The life of man and flower,
The wisdom and the energy
That fills the world with power.

3 Thou art the stream of love,
The unity divine;
Good men and true are one in thee,
And in thy radiance shine.

4 The heroes and the saints
Thy messengers became;
And all the lamps that guide the world
Were kindled at thy flame.

5 The calls that come to us
Upon thy winds are brought;
The light that gleams beyond our dreams
Is something thou hast thought.

6 Give fellowship, we pray,
In love and joy and peace,
That we in counsel, knowledge, might,
And wisdom, may increase.

Whitsuntide

90

Harriet Auber, 1773–1862.

OUR blest Redeemer, ere he breathed
His tender last farewell,
A Guide, a Comforter, bequeathed
With us to dwell.

2 He came in tongues of living flame,
To teach, convince, subdue;
All-powerful as the wind he came,
As viewless too.

3 He came sweet influence to impart,
A gracious, willing guest,
While he can find one humble heart
Wherein to rest.

4 And his that gentle voice we hear,
Soft as the breath of even,
That checks each fault, that calms each fear,
And speaks of heaven.

5 And every virtue we possess,
And every victory won,
And every thought of holiness,
Are his alone.

6 Spirit of purity and grace,
Our weakness, pitying, see:
O make our hearts thy dwelling-place,
And worthier thee.

91

Bianco da Siena, d. 1434.
Tr. R. F. Littledale.

COME down, O Love divine,
Seek thou this soul of mine,
And visit it with thine own ardour glowing;
O Comforter, draw near,
Within my heart appear,
And kindle it, thy holy flame bestowing.

2   O let it freely burn,
      Till earthly passions turn
To dust and ashes in its heat consuming;
    And let thy glorious light
    Shine ever on my sight,
And clothe me round, the while my path illuming.

3   Let holy charity
      Mine outward vesture be,
And lowliness become mine inner clothing;
    True lowliness of heart,
    Which takes the humbler part,
And o'er its own shortcomings weeps with loathing.

4   And so the yearning strong,
      With which the soul will long,
Shall far outpass the power of human telling;
    For none can guess its grace,
    Till he become the place
Wherein the Holy Spirit makes his dwelling.

92   *Foundling Hospital Collection* (1774).

SPIRIT of mercy, truth, and love,
  Shed thy blest influence from above,
And still from age to age convey
The wonders of this sacred day.

2 In every clime, in every tongue,
Be God's eternal praises sung;
Through all the listening earth be taught
The acts our great Redeemer wrought.

3 Unfailing Comfort, heavenly Guide,
Over thy favoured Church preside;
Still may mankind thy blessings prove,
Spirit of mercy, truth, and love.

93 *Scripture.*   *G. W. Briggs*, 1875–1959.

THE Spirit of the Lord revealed
  His will to saints of old,
Their heart and mind and lips unsealed
  His glory to unfold:

> In gloom of ancient night
> They witnessed to the dawning word,
> And in the coming of the light
> Proclaimed the coming Lord.

2 The prophets passed: at length there came,
To sojourn and abide,
The Word incarnate, to whose name
The prophets testified:
The twilight overpast,
Himself the very Light of light,
As man with men, revealed at last
The Father to our sight.

3 Eternal Spirit, who dost speak
To mind and conscience still,
That we, in this our day, may seek
To do our Father's will:
Thy word of life impart,
That tells of Christ, the living Way;
Give us the quiet humble heart
To hear and to obey.

THANKSGIVING

THE CHURCH: THE FAMILY OF GOD

94 *J. M. Neale, 1818–66.*

AROUND the throne of God a band
Of glorious angels always stand;
Bright things they see, sweet harps they hold,
And on their heads are crowns of gold!

2 Some wait around him, ready still
To sing his praise and do his will;
And some, when he commands them, go
To guard his servants here below.

3 Lord, give thy angels every day
Command to guide us on our way,
And bid them every evening keep
Their watch around us while we sleep.

4 So shall no wicked thing draw near,
　　To do us harm or cause us fear;
And we shall dwell, when life is past,
　　With angels round thy throne at last.

95   *Bishop R. Mant, 1776–1848.*

BRIGHT the vision that delighted
　　Once the sight of Judah's seer;
Sweet the countless tongues united
　　To entrance the prophet's ear.

2 Round the Lord in glory seated,
　　　Cherubim and seraphim
Filled his temple, and repeated
　　　Each to each the alternate hymn:

3 'Lord, thy glory fills the heaven;
　　　Earth is with its fullness stored;
Unto thee be glory given,
　　　Holy, holy, holy, Lord.'

4 Heaven is still with glory ringing,
　　　Earth takes up the angels' cry,
'Holy, holy, holy,' singing,
　　　'Lord of hosts, the Lord most high.'

96   *S. Johnson, 1822–82.*

CITY of God, how broad and far
　　Outspread thy walls sublime!
The true thy chartered freemen are
　　Of every age and clime.

2 One holy Church, one army strong,
　　　One steadfast, high intent;
One working band, one harvest-song,
　　　One King omnipotent.

3 How purely hath thy speech come down
　　From man's primeval youth!
How grandly hath thine empire grown
　　Of freedom, love and truth!

4 How gleam thy watch-fires through the night
    With never-fainting ray!
How rise thy towers, serene and bright,
    To meet the dawning day!

5 In vain the surge's angry shock,
    In vain the drifting sands:
Unharmed upon the eternal Rock
    The eternal City stands.

THE CHURCH IN HEAVEN AND EARTH

97 *Bishop W. W. How, 1823–97.*

The Communion of Saints.

F OR all the Saints who from their labours rest,
    Who thee by faith before the world confest,
Thy name, O Jesus, be for ever blest:
        Alleluya! Alleluya!

2 Thou wast their rock, their fortress, and their
    might;
Thou, Lord, their captain in the well-fought fight;
Thou in the darkness drear their one true light:
        Alleluya!

3 O may thy soldiers, faithful, true, and bold,
Fight as the saints who nobly fought of old,
And win, with them, the victor's crown of gold:
        Alleluya!

*4 O blest communion! fellowship divine!
We feebly struggle, they in glory shine;
Yet all are one in thee, for all are thine:
        Alleluya!

5 And when the strife is fierce, the warfare long,
Steals on the ear the distant triumph-song,
And hearts are brave again, and arms are strong:
        Alleluya!

6 The golden evening brightens in the west;
Soon, soon to faithful warriors cometh rest;
Sweet is the calm of paradise the blest:
        Alleluya!

*7 But lo! there breaks a yet more glorious day;
The saints triumphant rise in bright array:
The King of Glory passes on his way:
Alleluya!

*8 From earth's wide bounds, from ocean's farthest
coast,
Through gates of pearl streams in the countless
host,
Singing to Father, Son, and Holy Ghost:
Alleluya!

98   *W. Charter Piggott, 1872–1943.*

FOR those we love within the veil,
Who once were comrades of our way,
We thank thee, Lord; for they have won
To cloudless day;

2 And life for them is life indeed,
The splendid goal of earth's strait race;
And where no shadows intervene
They see thy face.

3 Not as we knew them any more,
Toilworn, and sad with burdened care,—
Erect, clear-eyed, upon their brows
Thy name they bear.

4 Free from the fret of mortal years,
And knowing now thy perfect will,
With quickened sense and heightened joy,
They serve thee still.

5 O fuller, sweeter is that life,
And larger, ampler, is the air.
Eye cannot see nor heart conceive
The glory there;

6 Nor know to what high purpose thou
Dost yet employ their ripened powers,
Nor how at thy behest they touch
This life of ours.

7 There are no tears within their eyes;
With thy love they keep perpetual tryst;
And praise and work and rest are one
    With thee, O Christ.

99
          George Herbert, 1593–1632.

LET all the world in every corner sing,
  My God and King!
  The heavens are not too high,
  His praise may thither fly;
  The earth is not too low,
  His praises there may grow.
Let all the world in every corner sing,
    My God and King!

2 Let all the world in every corner sing,
  My God and King!
  The Church with psalms must shout,
  No door can keep them out;
  But above all, the heart
  Must bear the longest part.
Let all the world in every corner sing,
    My God and King!

(*The first verse can be repeated, if desired.*)

100
          J. Newton, 1725–1807.

GLORIOUS things of thee are spoken,
  Sion, city of our God!
He whose word cannot be broken
  Formed thee for his own abode;
On the Rock of Ages founded,
  What can shake thy sure repose?
With salvation's walls surrounded,
  Thou may'st smile at all thy foes.

2 See, the streams of living waters,
  Springing from eternal love,
Well supply thy sons and daughters,
  And all fear of want remove.

Who can faint while such a river
  Ever flows their thirst to assuage,—
Grace which, like the Lord the Giver,
  Never fails from age to age?

3 Saviour, if of Sion's city
  I, through grace, a member am,
Let the world deride or pity,
  I will glory in thy name:
Fading is the worldling's pleasure,
  All his boasted pomp and show;
Solid joys and lasting treasure
  None but Sion's children know.

101   *F. T. Palgrave*, 1824–97.

O THOU not made with hands,
  Not throned above the skies,
Nor walled with shining walls,
  Nor framed with stones of price,
More bright than gold or gem,
God's own Jerusalem!

2 Where'er the gentle heart
  Finds courage from above;
Where'er the heart forsook
  Warms with the breath of love;
Where faith bids fear depart,
City of God, thou art.

3 Thou art where'er the proud
  In humbleness melts down;
Where self itself yields up;
  Where martyrs win their crown;
Where faithful souls possess
  Themselves in perfect peace;

4 Where in life's common ways
  With cheerful feet we go;
Where in his steps we tread,
  Who trod the way of woe;
Where he is in the heart,
City of God, thou art.

*5 Not throned above the skies,
　　Nor golden-walled afar,
　But where Christ's two or three
　　In his name gathered are,
　Be in the midst of them,
　God's own Jerusalem.

102
J. Montgomery,† 1771–1854.

SONGS of praise the angels sang,
　Heaven with alleluyas rang,
When creation was begun,
When God spake and it was done.

2 Songs of praise awoke the morn
　When the Prince of Peace was born:
Songs of praise arose when he
Captive led captivity.

*3 Heaven and earth must pass away,
　Songs of praise shall crown that day;
God will make new heavens and earth,
Songs of praise shall hail their birth.

*4 And will man alone be dumb
　Till that glorious kingdom come?
No, the Church delights to raise
Psalms and hymns and songs of praise.

5 Saints below, with heart and voice,
　Still in songs of praise rejoice,
Learning here by faith and love
Songs of praise to sing above.

6 Hymns of glory, songs of praise,
　Father, unto thee we raise;
Jesus, glory unto thee,
With the Spirit ever be.

103
I. Watts, 1674–1748.

THERE is a land of pure delight,
　Where Saints immortal reign;
Infinite day excludes the night,
　And pleasures banish pain.

2 There everlasting spring abides,
   And never-withering flowers;
   Death, like a narrow sea, divides
   This heavenly land from ours.

3 Sweet fields beyond the swelling flood
   Stand dressed in living green;
   So to the Jews old Canaan stood,
   While Jordan rolled between.

4 But timorous mortals start and shrink
   To cross this narrow sea,
   And linger shivering on the brink,
   And fear to launch away.

*5 O could we make our doubts remove,
   These gloomy doubts that rise,
   And see the Canaan that we love
   With unbeclouded eyes;

6 Could we but climb where Moses stood,
   And view the landscape o'er,
   Not Jordan's stream, nor death's cold flood,
   Should fright us from the shore!

104   *H. T. Schenk, 1656–1727. Tr. F. E. Cox.*

WHO are these, like stars appearing,
   These before God's throne who stand?
Each a golden crown is wearing;
   Who are all this glorious band?
      Alleluya, hark! they sing,
      Praising loud their heavenly king.

2 Who are these of dazzling brightness,
   These in God's own truth arrayed,
Clad in robes of purest whiteness,
   Robes whose lustre ne'er shall fade,
      Ne'er be touched by time's rude hand—
      Whence comes all this glorious band?

3 These are they who have contended
    For their Saviour's honour long,
Wrestling on till life was ended,
    Following not the sinful throng;
      These, who well the fight sustained,
      Triumph through the Lamb have gained.

*4 These are they whose hearts were riven,
    Sore with woe and anguish tried,
Who in prayer full oft have striven
    With the God they glorified;
      Now, their painful conflict o'er,
      God has bid them weep no more.

*5 These like priests have watched and waited,
    Offering up to Christ their will,
Soul and body consecrated,
    Day and night to serve him still:
      Now, in God's most holy place
      Blest they stand before his face.

105
                R. Baxter (1681), *and*
                J. H. Gurney (1838 *and* 1851).

YE holy angels bright,
    Who wait at God's right hand,
Or through the realms of light
    Fly at your Lord's command,
      Assist our song,
        For else the theme
        Too high doth seem
      For mortal tongue.

2 Ye blessèd souls at rest,
    Who ran this earthly race,
And now, from care released,
    Behold the Saviour's face,
      God's praises sound,
        As in his sight
        With sweet delight
      Ye do abound.

3 Ye saints, who toil below,
   Adore your heavenly King,
And onward as ye go
   Some joyful anthem sing;
     Take what he gives
      And praise him still,
      Through good or ill,
     Who ever lives.

4 My soul, bear thou thy part,
   Triumph in God above:
And with a well-tuned heart
   Sing thou the songs of love!
     Let all thy days
      Till life shall end,
      Whate'er he send,
     Be filled with praise.

NATURE: THE HANDIWORK OF GOD

Spring

106
                        G. W. Briggs, 1875–1959.

HARK! a hundred notes are swelling
    Loud and clear.
'Tis the happy birds are telling
    Spring is here!
Nature, decked in brave array,
Casts her winter robes away;
All earth's little folk rejoicing
   Haste to greet the glad new day.

2 Lord and life of all things living,
    Come to me:
Thou delightest but in giving;
    Give to me:
Spring of joyous life thou art:
Thine own joy to me impart:
Let my praises be the outburst
   Of the springtime in my heart.

107   *Jan Struther*, 1901-53.

SING, all ye Christian people!
  Swing, bells, in every steeple!
    For Christ to life is risen,
    Set free from death's dark prison.
With joyfulness, with joyfulness your alleluyas sing,
For Christ has come again to greet the spring.

2 Green now is on the larches;
Springtime in triumph marches,
    And every day uncloses
    A host of new primroses:
Then daffodils and marybuds let us in garlands
    bring,
For Christ has come again to greet the spring.

3 Skylarks, the earth forsaking,
Soar to their music-making,
    And in the roof-tree's hollow
    Now builds the trusting swallow:
So cries to him, so flies to him my soul on fearless
    wing,
For Christ has come again to greet the spring.

Summer

108   *Bishop Walsham How*, 1823-97.

SUMMER suns are glowing
  Over land and sea,
Happy light is flowing
  Bountiful and free.
Everything rejoices
  In the mellow rays,
All earth's thousand voices
  Swell the psalm of praise.

2 God's free mercy streameth
  Over all the world,
And his banner gleameth
  Everywhere unfurled.

Broad and deep and glorious
    As the heaven above,
Shines in might victorious
    His eternal love.

3 Lord, upon our blindness
    Thy pure radiance pour;
For thy loving-kindness
    Make us love thee more.
And when clouds are drifting
    Dark across our sky,
Then, the veil uplifting,
    Father, be thou nigh.

4 We will never doubt thee,
    Though thou veil thy light:
Life is dark without thee;
    Death with thee is bright.
Light of light! Shine o'er us
    On our pilgrim way,
Go thou still before us
    To the endless day.

Harvest

109   H. Alford,‡ 1810–71.

COME, ye thankful people, come,
    Raise the song of harvest-home!
All be safely gathered in,
Ere the winter storms begin;
God, our Maker, doth provide
For our wants to be supplied;
Come to God's own temple, come;
Raise the song of harvest-home!

2 All this world is God's own field,
Fruit unto his praise to yield;
Wheat and tares together sown,
Unto joy or sorrow grown;
First the blade and then the ear,
Then the full corn shall appear:
Lord of harvest, grant that we
Wholesome grain and pure may be.

3 For the Lord our God shall come,
  And shall take his harvest home;
From his field shall purge away
  All that doth offend to-day;
Give his angels charge at last
In the fire the tares to cast,
  But the fruitful wheat to store
  In his barn for evermore.

*4 Then, thou Church triumphant, come,
  Raise the song of harvest-home;
All be safely gathered in,
  Free from sorrow, free from sin,
Therefore ever purified
in God's garner to abide:
  Come, ten thousand angels, come,
  Raise the glorious harvest-home!

110 *Ps.* 136.   *J. Milton,* 1608–74.

L ET us, with a gladsome mind,
  Praise the Lord, for he is kind:
    For his mercies ay endure,
    Ever faithful, ever sure.

2 Let us blaze his name abroad,
  For of gods he is the God:

3 He with all-commanding might
  Filled the new-made world with light:

*4 He the golden-tressèd sun
  Caused all day his course to run:

*5 The hornèd moon to shine by night,
  'Mid her spangled sisters bright:

6 All things living he doth feed,
  His full hand supplies their need:

7 Let us, with a gladsome mind,
  Praise the Lord, for he is kind:
    For his mercies ay endure,
    Ever faithful, ever sure.

111

M. Claudius, 1740–1815.
Tr. J. M. Campbell.

WE plough the fields, and scatter
　　The good seed on the land,
But it is fed and watered
　　By God's almighty hand:
He sends the snow in winter,
　　The warmth to swell the grain,
The breezes and the sunshine,
　　And soft refreshing rain:
　　　　All good gifts around us
　　　　　Are sent from heaven above;
　　　　Then thank the Lord, O thank the Lord,
　　　　　For all his love.

2 He only is the Maker
　　Of all things near and far,
He paints the wayside flower,
　　He lights the evening star.
The winds and waves obey him,
　　By him the birds are fed;
Much more to us, his children,
　　He gives our daily bread:

3 We thank thee then, O Father,
　　For all things bright and good;
The seed-time and the harvest,
　　Our life, our health, our food.
No gifts have we to offer
　　For all thy love imparts,
But that which thou desirest,
　　Our humble, thankful hearts:
　　　　All good gifts around us
　　　　　Are sent from heaven above;
　　　　Then thank the Lord, O thank the Lord,
　　　　　For all his love.

112　*Treasure.*　　　　*Jan Struther, 1901–53.*

DAISIES are our silver,
　　Buttercups our gold:
This is all the treasure
　　We can have or hold.

2 Raindrops are our diamonds
   And the morning dew;
While for shining sapphires
   We've the speedwell blue.

3 These shall be our emeralds—
   Leaves so new and green;
Roses make the reddest
   Rubies ever seen.

4 God, who gave these treasures
   To your children small,
Teach us how to love them
   And grow like them all.

5 Make us bright as silver:
   Make us good as gold;
Warm as summer roses
   Let our hearts unfold.

6 Gay as leaves in April,
   Clear as drops of dew—
God, who made the speedwell,
   Keep us true to you.

113   *F. S. Pierpoint,*† 1835–1917.

FOR the beauty of the earth,
   For the beauty of the skies,
For the love which from our birth
   Over and around us lies:
      Father, unto thee we raise
      This our sacrifice of praise.

2 For the beauty of each hour
   Of the day and of the night,
Hill and vale, and tree and flower,
   Sun and moon and stars of light:

3 For the joy of ear and eye,
   For the heart and brain's delight,
For the mystic harmony
   Linking sense to sound and sight:

4 For the joy of human love,
　　Brother, sister, parent, child,
　Friends on earth, and friends above,
　　For all gentle thoughts and mild:

5 For each perfect gift of thine
　　To our race so freely given,
　Graces human and divine,
　　Flowers of earth and buds of heaven:
　　　Father, unto thee we raise
　　　This our sacrifice of praise.

114　　　　　*Lizette Woodworth Reese*, 1856–1935.

G LAD that I live am I;
　　That the sky is blue;
　Glad for the country lanes,
　And the fall of dew.

2 After the sun the rain,
　After the rain the sun;
　This is the way of life,
　Till the work be done.

3 All that we need to do,
　Be we low or high,
　Is to see that we grow
　Nearer the sky.

115　　　　　*Bishop Cotton*, 1813–66.

W E thank thee, Lord, for this fair earth,
　　The glittering sky, the silver sea;
　For all their beauty, all their worth,
　　Their light and glory, come from thee.

2 Thanks for the flowers that clothe the ground,
　　The trees that wave their arms above,
　The hills that gird our dwellings round,
　　As thou dost gird thine own with love.

3 Yet teach us still how far more fair,
　　More glorious, Father, in thy sight,
　Is one pure deed, one holy prayer,
　　One heart that owns thy Spirit's might.

4 So, while we gaze with thoughtful eye
   On all the gifts thy love has given,
Help us in thee to live and die,
   By thee to rise from earth to heaven.

116   *Jan Struther*, 1901–53.

WE thank you, Lord of Heaven,
   For all the joys that greet us,
For all that you have given
   To help us and delight us
      In earth and sky and seas;
The sunlight on the meadows,
   The rainbow's fleeting wonder,
The clouds with cooling shadows,
    The stars that shine in splendour—
      We thank you, Lord, for these.

2 For swift and gallant horses,
   For lambs in pastures springing,
For dogs with friendly faces,
   For birds with music thronging
      Their chantries in the trees;
For herbs to cool our fever,
   For flowers of field and garden,
For bees among the clover
    With stolen sweetness laden—
      We thank you, Lord, for these.

3 For homely dwelling-places
   Where childhood's visions linger,
For friends and kindly voices,
   For bread to stay our hunger
      And sleep to bring us ease;
For zeal and zest of living,
   For faith and understanding,
For words to tell our loving,
    For hope of peace unending—
      We thank you, Lord, for these.

Winter

117   P. Dearmer, 1867–1936.

WINTER creeps, Nature sleeps;
  Birds are gone, Flowers are none,
Fields are bare, Bleak the air,
Leaves are shed: All seems dead.

2 God's alive! Grow and thrive,
Hidden away, Bloom of May,
Robe of June! Very soon
Nought but green Will be seen!

(For Nature Hymns see also 16–19, 21, 22, 27.)

GENERAL

118   George Herbert, 1593–1632.

KING of glory, King of peace,
      I will love thee;
And that love may never cease,
      I will move thee.
Thou hast granted my request,
      Thou hast heard me;
Thou didst note my working breast,
      Thou hast spared me.

2 Wherefore with my utmost art
      I will sing thee,
And the cream of all my heart
      I will bring thee.
Though my sins against me cried,
      Thou didst clear me;
And alone, when they replied,
      Thou didst hear me.

3 Seven whole days, not one in seven,
      I will praise thee;
In my heart, though not in heaven,
      I can raise thee.
Small it is, in this poor sort
      To enrol thee:
E'en eternity's too short
      To extol thee.

(For little children)

119 *Praise.*   *Songs of Praise version.*

PRAISE him, praise him, all his children praise
    him.
  He is love, he is love.

2 Thank him, thank him, all his children thank him!
  He is love, he is love.

3 Love him, love him, all his children love him!
  He is love, he is love.

4 Crown him, crown him, all his children crown him!
  He is love, he is love.

120   *R. Bridges, 1844–1930.*

REJOICE, O land, in God thy might,
  His will obey, him serve aright;
  For thee the Saints uplift their voice:
  Fear not, O land, in God rejoice.

2 Glad shalt thou be, with blessing crowned,
  With joy and peace thou shalt abound;
  Yea, love with thee shall make his home
  Until thou see God's kingdom come.

3 He shall forgive thy sins untold:
  Remember thou his love of old;
  Walk in his way, his word adore,
  And keep his truth for evermore.

121   *I. Watts, 1674–1748.*

FROM all that dwell below the skies
  Let the Creator's praise arise:
  Let the Redeemer's name be sung
  Through every land by every tongue.

2 Eternal are thy mercies, Lord,
  Eternal truth attends thy word:
  Thy praise shall sound from shore to shore,
  Till suns shall rise and set no more.

122

Charles Wesley, 1707-88.

REJOICE, the Lord is King,
  Your Lord and King adore;
Mortals give thanks and sing,
  And triumph evermore:
    Lift up your heart, lift up your voice;
    Rejoice, again I say, rejoice.

2 Jesus, the Saviour, reigns,
    The God of truth and love;
  When he had purged our stains,
    He took his seat above:

3 His kingdom cannot fail;
    He rules o'er earth and heaven;
  The keys of death and hell
    Are to our Jesus given:

4 He sits at God's right hand
    Till all his foes submit,
  And bow to his command,
    And fall beneath his feet:
      Lift up your heart, lift up your voice;
      Rejoice, again I say, rejoice.

PRAYER

123

Mrs. L. M. Willis, 1824-1908.

FATHER, hear the prayer we offer;
  Not for ease that prayer shall be,
But for strength that we may ever
  Live our lives courageously.

2 Not for ever in green pastures
    Do we ask our way to be;
  But the steep and rugged pathway
    May we tread rejoicingly.

3 Not for ever by still waters
    Would we idly rest and stay;
  But would smite the living fountains
    From the rocks along our way.

4 Be our strength in hours of weakness,
　In our wanderings be our guide;
Through endeavour, failure, danger,
　Father, be thou at our side.

124
　　　　　　　　　　　G. Thring, 1823–1903.

FIERCE raged the tempest o'er the deep,
　Watch did thine anxious servants keep,
But thou wast wrapped in guileless sleep,
　　　　　Calm and still.

2 'Save, Lord, we perish!' was their cry,
　'O save us in our agony!'
Thy word above the storm rose high,
　　　　　　'Peace, be still.'

3 The wild winds hushed; the angry deep
　Sank, like a little child, to sleep;
The sullen billows ceased to leap,
　　　　　At thy will.

4 So, when our life is clouded o'er,
　And storm-winds drift us from the shore,
Say, lest we sink to rise no more,
　　　　　　'Peace, be still.'

125
　　　　　　　　　　P. Dearmer, 1867–1936.

JESUS, good above all other,
　Gentle Child of gentle mother,
In a stable born our Brother,
　　　　　Give us grace to persevere.

2 Jesus, cradled in a manger,
　For us facing every danger,
Living as a homeless stranger,
　　　　　Make we thee our King most dear.

3 Jesus, for thy people dying,
　Risen Master, death defying,
Lord in heaven, thy grace supplying,
　　　　　Keep us to thy presence near.

4 Jesus, who our sorrows bearest,
All our thoughts and hopes thou sharest,
Thou to man the truth declarest;
    Help us all thy truth to hear.

5 Lord, in all our doings guide us;
Pride and hate shall ne'er divide us;
We'll go on with thee beside us,
    And with joy we'll persevere!

Unity

126
         Charles Wesley, 1707–88.

JESUS, Lord, we look to thee;
  Let us in thy name agree;
Show thyself the Prince of Peace;
Bid our strife for ever cease.

2 Make us of one heart and mind,
Courteous, pitiful, and kind,
Lowly, meek, in thought and word,
Altogether like our Lord.

3 Let us each for other care,
Each the other's burden bear,
To thy Church the pattern give,
Show how true believers live.

4 Free from anger and from pride,
Let us thus in God abide;
All the depths of love express,
All the height of holiness.

127
         W. Cowper, 1731–1800.

JESUS, where'er thy people meet,
  There they behold thy mercy-seat;
Where'er they seek thee, thou art found,
And every place is hallowed ground.

2 For thou, within no walls confined,
Inhabitest the humble mind;
Such ever bring thee where they come,
And going, take thee to their home.

3 Dear Shepherd of thy chosen few,
  Thy former mercies here renew;
Here to our waiting hearts proclaim
  The sweetness of thy saving name.

4 Here may we prove the power of prayer,
  To strengthen faith and sweeten care;
To teach our faint desires to rise,
  And bring all heaven before our eyes.

5 Lord, we are few, but thou art near;
  Nor short thine arm, nor deaf thine ear;
O rend the heavens, come quickly down,
  And make a thousand hearts thine own!

128   *J. R. Wreford*, 1800–81.

LORD, while for all mankind we pray
  Of every clime and coast,
O hear us for our native land,
  The land we love the most.

2 O guard our shores from every foe;
  With peace our borders bless;
With prosperous times our cities crown,
  Our fields with plenteousness.

3 Unite us in the sacred love
  Of knowledge, truth, and thee;
And let our hills and valleys shout
  The songs of liberty.

4 Lord of the nations, thus to thee
  Our country we commend;
Be thou her refuge and her trust,
  Her everlasting friend.

129   *C. Wesley*, 1707–88.

O FOR a heart to praise my God,
  A heart from sin set free:
A heart that always feels thy blood
  So freely spilt for me;

2 A heart resigned, submissive, meek,
My dear Redeemer's throne;
Where only Christ is heard to speak,
Where Jesus reigns alone:

3 A humble, lowly, contrite heart,
Believing, true, and clean,
Which neither life nor death can part
From him that dwells within:

4 A heart in every thought renewed,
And full of love divine;
Perfect, and right, and pure, and good,
A copy, Lord, of thine.

5 Thy nature, gracious Lord, impart,
Come quickly from above;
Write thy new name upon my heart,
Thy new best name of Love.

130 *Scottish Psalter* (1650).

PRAY that Jerusalem may have
Peace and felicity:
Let them that love thee and thy peace
Have still prosperity.

2 Behold how good a thing it is,
And how becoming well,
Together such as brethren are
In unity to dwell.

3 Therefore I wish that peace may still
Within thy walls remain,
And ever may thy palaces
Prosperity retain.

4 Now, for my friends' and brethren's sake,
Peace be in thee, I'll say;
And for the house of God our Lord
I'll seek thy good alway.

131 *Mrs. J. C. Simpson, 1811–86, and others.*

PRAY when the morn is breaking,
　Pray when the noon is bright,
Pray with the eve's declining,
　Pray in the hush of night:
With mind made clear of tumult,
　All meaner thoughts away,
Make thou thy soul transparent,
　Seek thou with God to pray.

2 Remember all who love thee,
　All who are loved by thee,
And next for those that hate thee
　Pray thou, if such there be:
Last for thyself in meekness
　A blessing humbly claim,
And link with each petition
　Thy great Redeemer's name.

3 But if 'tis e'er denied thee
　In solitude to pray,
Should holy thoughts come o'er thee
　Upon life's crowded way,
E'en then the silent breathing
　That lifts thy soul above
Shall reach the thronèd Presence
　Of mercy, truth, and love.

132 *J. Montgomery, 1771–1854.*

PRAYER is the soul's sincere desire,
　Uttered or unexpressed;
The motion of a hidden fire
　That trembles in the breast.

2 Prayer is the burden of a sigh,
　The falling of a tear,
The upward glancing of an eye
　When none but God is near.

3 Prayer is the simplest form of speech
   That infant lips can try;
Prayer the sublimest strains that reach
   The Majesty on high.

4 Prayer is the contrite sinner's voice,
   Returning from his ways,
While angels in their songs rejoice,
   And cry, 'Behold, he prays!'

5 Prayer is the Christian's vital breath,
   The Christian's native air,
His watchword at the gates of death:
   He enters heaven with prayer.

6 O thou by whom we come to God,
   The Life, the Truth, the Way,
The path of prayer thyself hast trod:
   Lord, teach us how to pray.

133   *Jane E. Leeson*, 1807–82.

SAVIOUR, teach me, day by day,
   Love's sweet lesson to obey;
Sweeter lesson cannot be,
   Loving him who first loved me.

2 With a child's glad heart of love
   At thy bidding may I move,
Prompt to serve and follow thee,
   Loving him who first loved me.

3 Teach me thus thy steps to trace,
   Strong to follow in thy grace,
Learning how to love from thee,
   Loving him who so loved me.

4 Love in loving finds employ,
   In obedience all her joy;
Ever new that joy will be,
   Loving him who first loved me.

THE SPREAD OF THE KINGDOM

134
P. Dearmer, 1867–1936.

A BRIGHTER dawn is breaking,
  And earth with praise is waking;
For thou, O King most highest,
The power of death defiest;

2 And thou hast come victorious,
  With risen body glorious,
Who now for ever livest,
And life abundant givest.

3 O free the world from blindness,
  And fill the world with kindness,
Give sinner resurrection,
Bring striving to perfection;

4 In sickness give us healing,
  In doubt thy clear revealing,
That praise to thee be given
In earth as in thy heaven.

135
Basil Mathews, 1879–1951.

F AR round the world thy children sing their
      song;
  From East and West their voices sweetly blend,
Praising the Lord in whom young lives are strong,
  Jesus our guide, our hero, and our friend.

*2 Guide of the pilgrim clambering to the height,
  Hero on whom our fearful hearts depend,
Friend of the wanderer yearning for the light,
  Jesus our guide, our hero, and our friend.

3 Where thy wide ocean, wave on rolling wave,
  Beats through the ages on each island shore,
They praise their Lord, whose hand alone can
      save,
  Whose sea of love surrounds them evermore.

4 Thy sun-kissed children on earth's spreading plain,
  Where Asia's rivers water all the land,
Sing, as they watch thy fields of glowing grain,
  Praise to the Lord who feeds them with his
      hand.

5 Still there are lands where none have seen thy face,
  Children whose hearts have never shared thy joy:
Yet thou would'st pour on these thy radiant grace,
  Give thy glad strength to every girl and boy.

*6 All round the world let children sing thy song,
  From East and West their voices sweetly blend;
Praising the Lord in whom young lives are strong,
  Jesus our guide, our hero, and our friend.

136
G. Thring, 1823–1903.

FROM the eastern mountains
    Pressing on they come,
Wise men in their wisdom,
    To his humble home;
Stirred by deep devotion,
    Hasting from afar,
Ever journeying onward,
    Guided by a star.

2 There their Lord and Saviour
    Meek and lowly lay,
Wondrous light that led them
    Onward on their way,
Ever now to lighten
    Nations from afar,
As they journey homeward
    By that guiding star.

3 Thou who in a manger
    Once hast lowly lain,
Who dost now in glory
    O'er all kingdoms reign,
Gather in the heathen,
    Who in lands afar
Ne'er have seen the brightness
    Of thy guiding star.

4 Gather in the outcasts,
  All who've gone astray;
Throw thy radiance o'er them,
  Guide them on their way;
Those who never knew thee,
  Those who've wandered far,
Guide them by the brightness
  Of thy guiding star.

*5 Onward through the darkness
  Of the lonely night,
Shining still before them
  With thy kindly light,
Guide them, Jew and Gentile,
  Homeward from afar,
Young and old together,
  By thy guiding star.

*6 Until every nation,
  Whether bond or free,
'Neath thy star-lit banner,
  Jesus, follows thee,
O'er the distant mountains
  To that heavenly home
Where nor sin nor sorrow
  Evermore shall come.

137   *Charles E. Oakley, 1832–65.*

HILLS of the North, rejoice;
  River and mountain-spring,
Hark to the advent voice;
  Valley and lowland, sing;
Though absent long, your Lord is nigh;
He judgement brings and victory.

2   Isles of the Southern Seas,
      Deep in your coral caves
   Pent be each warring breeze,
      Lulled be your restless waves:
   He comes to reign with boundless sway,
   And makes your wastes his great highway.

3   Lands of the East, awake,
        Soon shall your sons be free;
    The sleep of ages break,
        And rise to liberty.
    On your far hills, long cold and grey,
    Has dawned the everlasting day.

4   Shores of the utmost West,
        Ye that have waited long,
    Unvisited, unblest,
        Break forth to swelling song;
    High raise the note, that Jesus died,
    Yet lives and reigns, the Crucified.

*5   Shout, while ye journey home;
        Songs be in every mouth;
    Lo, from the North we come,
        From East, and West, and South.
    City of God, the bond are free,
    We come to live and reign in thee!

138   *I. Watts*, 1674–1748.

JESUS shall reign where'er the sun
    Does his successive journeys run;
His kingdom stretch from shore to shore,
Till moons shall wax and wane no more.

2 People and realms of every tongue
    Dwell on his love with sweetest song,
And infant voices shall proclaim
    Their early blessings on his name.

3 Blessings abound where'er he reigns;
    The prisoner leaps to lose his chains;
The weary find eternal rest,
    And all the sons of want are blest.

4 Let every creature rise and bring
    Peculiar honours to our King;
Angels descend with songs again,
    And earth repeat the long amen.

139

S. Baring-Gould, 1834–1924.

ONWARD, Christian soldiers,
  Marching as to war,
With the cross of Jesus
  Going on before.
Christ the royal Master
  Leads against the foe;
Forward into battle,
  See his banners go!

  Onward, Christian soldiers,
    Marching as to war,
  With the cross of Jesus
    Going on before.

2 Like a mighty army
    Moves the Church of God;
  Brothers, we are treading
    Where the saints have trod;
  We are not divided,
    All one body we,
  One in hope and doctrine,
    One in charity:

3 Crowns and thrones may perish,
    Kingdoms rise and wane,
  But the Church of Jesus
    Constant will remain;
  Gates of hell can never
    'Gainst that Church prevail;
  We have Christ's own promise,
    And that cannot fail:

4 Onward, then, ye people,
    Join our happy throng,
  Blend with ours your voices
    In the triumph song;
  Glory, laud, and honour
    Unto Christ the King;
  This through countless ages
    Men and Angels sing:

Onward, Christian soldiers,
Marching as to war,
With the cross of Jesus
Going on before.

140
P. Dearmer, 1867–1936.

REMEMBER all the people
Who live in far-off lands
In strange and lovely cities,
  Or roam the desert sands,
Or farm the mountain pastures,
  Or till the endless plains
Where children wade through rice fields
  And watch the camel trains:

2 Some work in sultry forests
  Where apes swing to and fro,
Some fish in mighty rivers,
  Some hunt across the snow.
Remember all God's children,
  Who yet have never heard
The truth that comes from Jesus,
  The glory of his word.

3 God bless the men and women
  Who serve him overseas;
God raise up more to help them
  To set the nations free,
Till all the distant people
  In every foreign place
Shall understand his Kingdom
  And come into his grace.

141
G. Duffield,† 1818–88.

STAND up, stand up for Jesus,
  Ye soldiers of the cross!
Lift high his royal banner;
  It must not suffer loss.
From victory unto victory
  His army he shall lead,
Till every foe is vanquish'd,
  And Christ is Lord indeed.

2 Stand up, stand up for Jesus!
    Stand in his strength alone;
The arm of flesh will fail you,
    Ye dare not trust your own.
Put on the Gospel armour,
    Each piece put on with prayer;
Where duty calls or danger,
    Be never wanting there!

3 Stand up, stand up for Jesus!
    The strife will not be long;
This day the noise of battle,
    The next the victor's song.
To him that overcometh
    A crown of life shall be;
He with the King of Glory
    Shall reign eternally.

142   *Bishop R. Heber, 1783–1826*

THE Son of God goes forth to war,
    A kingly crown to gain;
His blood-red banner streams afar!
    Who follows in his train?
Who best can drink his cup of woe,
    Triumphant over pain,
Who patient bears his cross below,
    He follows in his train.

2 The Martyr first, whose eagle eye
    Could pierce beyond the grave;
Who saw his Master in the sky,
    And called on him to save.
Like him, with pardon on his tongue
    In midst of mortal pain,
He prayed for them that did the wrong!
    Who follows in his train?

3 A glorious band, the chosen few
    On whom the Spirit came,
Twelve valiant Saints, their hope they knew,
    And mocked the cross and flame.

They met the tyrant's brandish'd steel,
   The lion's gory mane,
They bowed their necks the death to feel;
   Who follows in their train?

4 A noble army, men and boys,
   The matron and the maid,
Around the Saviour's throne rejoice
   In robes of light arrayed.
They climbed the steep ascent of heaven
   Through peril, toil and pain;
O God, to us may grace be given
   To follow in their train.

143   *Jan Struther*, 1901–53.
WHEN a knight won his spurs, in the stories of
   old,
He was gentle and brave, he was gallant and bold;
With a shield on his arm and a lance in his hand
For God and for valour he rode through the land.

2 No charger have I, and no sword by my side,
Yet still to adventure and battle I ride,
Though back into storyland giants have fled,
And the knights are no more and the dragons are
   dead.

3 Let faith be my shield and let joy be my steed
'Gainst the dragons of anger, the ogres of greed;
And let me set free, with the sword of my youth,
From the castle of darkness the power of the truth.

(*For Missionary Hymns see also* 30, 96, 99.)

SPECIAL OCCASIONS
MORNING

144   *Bishop T. Ken*, 1637–1711.
AWAKE, my soul, and with the sun
   Thy daily stage of duty run;
Shake off dull sloth, and joyful rise
To pay thy morning sacrifice.

2 Let all thy converse be sincere
Thy conscience as the noon-day clear;
Think how all-seeing God thy ways
And all thy secret thoughts surveys.

3 Wake, and lift up thyself, my heart,
And with the Angels bear thy part,
Who all night long unwearied sing
High praise to the eternal King.

4 Praise God, from whom all blessings flow;
Praise him, all creatures here below;
Praise him above, ye heavenly host;
Praise Father, Son, and Holy Ghost. Amen.

145   *Charles Wesley, 1707–88.*

CHRIST, whose glory fills the skies,
 Christ, the true, the only Light,
Sun of Righteousness, arise,
 Triumph o'er the shades of night;
Dayspring from on high, be near;
Daystar, in my heart appear.

2 Dark and cheerless is the morn
 Unaccompanied by thee;
Joyless is the day's return,
 Till thy mercy's beams I see;
Till they inward light impart,
Glad my eyes, and warm my heart.

3 Visit then this soul of mine,
 Pierce the gloom of sin and grief;
Fill me, Radiancy divine,
 Scatter all my unbelief;
More and more thyself display,
Shining to the perfect day.

146   *Rebecca J. Weston (1885).*

FATHER, we thank thee for the night,
 And for the pleasant morning light;
For rest and food and loving care,
And all that makes the day so fair.

2 Help us to do the things we should,
  To be to others kind and good;
  In all we do at work or play
  To grow more loving every day.

147   *Eleanor Farjeon, 1881–1965.*

MORNING has broken
    Like the first morning,
Blackbird has spoken
    Like the first bird.
        Praise for the singing!
        Praise for the morning!
        Praise for them, springing
            Fresh from the Word!

2 Sweet the rain's new fall
    Sunlit from heaven,
Like the first dewfall
    On the first grass.
        Praise for the sweetness
        Of the wet garden,
        Sprung in completeness
            Where his feet pass.

3 Mine is the sunlight!
    Mine is the morning
Born of the one light
    Eden saw play!
        Praise with elation,
        Praise every morning,
        God's re-creation
            Of the new day!

148   *Thomas Carlyle, 1795–1881.*

SO here hath been dawning
    Another blue day:
Think, wilt thou let it
    Slip useless away?

2 Out of eternity
    This new day is born;
Into eternity,
    At night, will return.

3 Behold it aforetime
    No eye ever did:
So soon it forever
    From all eyes is hid.

4 Here hath been dawning
    Another blue day:
Think, wilt thou let it
    Slip useless away?

149

J. Keble, 1792–1866.

NEW every morning is the love
    Our wakening and uprising prove;
Through sleep and darkness safely brought,
Restored to life, and power, and thought.

2 New mercies, each returning day,
    Hover around us while we pray;
New perils past, new sins forgiven,
New thoughts of God, new hopes of heaven.

3 If on our daily course our mind
    Be set to hallow all we find,
New treasures still, of countless price,
God will provide for sacrifice.

4 The trivial round, the common task,
    Would furnish all we ought to ask,—
Room to deny ourselves, a road
To bring us daily nearer God.

5 Only, O Lord, in thy dear love
    Fit us for perfect rest above;
And help us this and every day
To live more nearly as we pray.

150   *Based on Robert Herrick, 1591–1674.*

WHEN virgin morn doth call thee to arise,
    Come thus in sober joy to sacrifice:

2 First wash thy heart in innocence, then bring
    Pure hands, pure habits; make pure everything.

3 Next humbly kneel before God's throne, and thence
    Give up thy soul in clouds of frankincense.

4 Censers of gold, thus filled with odours sweet,
    Shall make thy actions with their ends to meet.

EVENING

151   *Bishop T. Ken, 1637–1711.*

GLORY to thee, my God, this night
    For all the blessings of the light;
Keep me, O keep me, King of kings,
Beneath thy own almighty wings.

2 Forgive me, Lord, for thy dear Son,
    The ill that I this day have done,
    That with the world, myself, and thee,
    I, ere I sleep, at peace may be.

3 Teach me to live, that I may dread
    The grave as little as my bed;
    Teach me to die, that so I may
    Rise glorious at the awful day.

4 O may my soul on thee repose,
    And with sweet sleep mine eyelids close,
    Sleep that may me more vigorous make
    To serve my God when I awake.

5 Praise God, from whom all blessings flow;
    Praise him, all creatures here below;
    Praise him above, ye heavenly host;
    Praise Father, Son, and Holy Ghost. Amen.

152
1. *Bishop Heber* (1827).
2. *Archbishop Whately* (1855).

GOD, that madest earth and heaven,
   Darkness and light;
Who the day for toil hast given,
   For rest the night;
May thine angel guards defend us,
Slumber sweet thy mercy send us,
Holy dreams and hopes attend us,
   This livelong night.

2 Guard us waking, guard us sleeping;
      And, when we die,
May we in thy mighty keeping
      All peaceful lie:
So when death to life shall wake us,
Thou may'st like the angels make us,
And to reign in glory take us
      With thee on high.

153
S. Baring-Gould, 1834–1924.

NOW the day is over,
   Night is drawing nigh,
Shadows of the evening
   Steal across the sky.

2 Now the darkness gathers,
      Stars begin to peep,
Birds and beasts and flowers
      Soon will be asleep.

3 Jesus, give the weary
      Calm and sweet repose;
With thy tenderest blessing
      May mine eyelids close.

4 Grant to little children
      Visions bright of thee;
Guard the sailors tossing
      On the deep blue sea.

5 Comfort every sufferer
    Watching late in pain;
Those who plan some evil
    From their sin restrain.

*6 Through the long night watches
    May thine angels spread
Their white wings above me,
    Watching round my bed.

*7 When the morning wakens,
    Then may I arise
Pure, and fresh, and sinless
    In thy holy eyes.

8 Glory to the Father,
    Glory to the Son,
And to thee, blest Spirit,
    Whilst all ages run.

154   *W. Romanis*, 1824–99.

ROUND me falls the night;
    Saviour, be my light:
Through the hours in darkness shrouded
Let me see thy face unclouded;
    Let thy glory shine
    In this heart of mine.

2   Earthly work is done,
    Earthly sounds are none;
Rest in sleep and silence seeking,
Let me hear thee softly speaking;
    In my spirit's ear
    Whisper, 'I am near.'

3   Blessèd, heavenly Light,
    Shining through earth's night;
Voice, that oft of love hast told me;
Arms, so strong to clasp and hold me;
    Thou thy watch wilt keep,
    Saviour, o'er my sleep.

155

J. Ellerton, 1826–93.

SAVIOUR, again to thy dear name we raise
With one accord our parting hymn of praise.
Guard thou the lips from sin, the hearts from
shame,
That in this house have called upon thy name.

2 Grant us thy peace, Lord, through the coming
night;
Turn thou for us its darkness into light;
From harm and danger keep thy children free,
For dark and light are both alike to thee.

3 Grant us thy peace throughout our earthly life;
Peace to thy Church from error and from strife;
Peace to our land, the fruit of truth and love;
Peace in each heart, thy Spirit from above:

4 Thy peace in life, the balm of every pain;
Thy peace in death, the hope to rise again;
Then, when thy voice shall bid our conflict cease,
Call us, O Lord, to thine eternal peace.

156

J. Keble, 1792–1866.

SUN of my soul, thou Saviour dear,
It is not night if thou be near:
O may no earth-born cloud arise
To hide thee from thy servant's eyes.

2 When the soft dews of kindly sleep
My wearied eyelids gently steep,
Be my last thought, how sweet to rest
For ever on my Saviour's breast.

3 Abide with me from morn till eve,
For without thee I cannot live;
Abide with me when night is nigh,
For without thee I dare not die.

4 If some poor wandering child of thine
Have spurned to-day the voice divine,
Now, Lord, the gracious work begin;
Let him no more lie down in sin.

5 Watch by the sick; enrich the poor
With blessings from thy boundless store;
Be every mourner's sleep to-night
Like infant's slumbers, pure and light.

6 Come near and bless us when we wake,
Ere through the world our way we take;
Till in the ocean of thy love
We lose ourselves in heaven above.

157　　　*P. Gerhardt, 1607–76. Tr. R. Bridges.*

THE duteous day now closeth,
Each flower and tree reposeth,
　Shade creeps o'er wild and wood:
Let us, as night is falling,
On God our Maker calling,
　Give thanks to him, the Giver good.

2 Now all the heavenly splendour
Breaks forth in starlight tender
　From myriad worlds unknown;
And man, the marvel seeing,
Forgets his selfish being,
　For joy of beauty not his own.

3 His care he drowneth yonder,
Lost in the abyss of wonder;
　To heaven his soul doth steal:
This life he disesteemeth,
The day it is that dreameth,
　That doth from truth his vision seal.

4 Awhile his mortal blindness
May miss God's lovingkindness,
　And grope in faithless strife:
But when life's day is over
Shall death's fair night discover
　The fields of everlasting life.

158

M. M. Penstone,† 1859–1910.

WHEN lamps are lighted in the town,
 The boats sail out to sea;
The fishers watch when night comes down,
 They work for you and me.

2 When little children go to rest,
 Before they sleep, they pray
That God will bless the fishermen
 And bring them back at day.

3 The boats come in at early dawn,
 When children wake in bed;
Upon the beach the boats are drawn,
 And all the nets are spread.

4 God hath watched o'er the fishermen
 Far on the deep dark sea,
And brought them safely home again,
 Where they are glad to be.

HOSPITALS

159

E. H. Plumptre, 1821–91.

THINE arm, O Lord, in days of old
 Was strong to heal and save;
It triumphed o'er disease and death,
 O'er darkness and the grave;
To thee they went, the blind, the dumb,
 The palsied and the lame,
The leper with his tainted life,
 The sick with fevered frame.

2 And lo! thy touch brought life and health,
 Gave speech, and strength, and sight;
And youth renewed and frenzy calmed
 Owned thee the Lord of light;
And now, O Lord, be near to bless,
 Almighty as of yore,
In crowded street, by restless couch,
 As by Gennesareth's shore.

3 Be thou our great deliverer still,
  Thou Lord of life and death;
Restore and quicken, soothe and bless
  With thine almighty breath;
To hands that work, and eyes that see,
  Give wisdom's heavenly lore,
That whole and sick, and weak and strong,
  May praise thee evermore.

FOR THOSE AT SEA

160   *W. Whiting*, 1825–78.

ETERNAL Father, strong to save,
  Whose arm doth bind the restless wave,
Who bidd'st the mighty ocean deep
Its own appointed limits keep:
    O hear us when we cry to thee
    For those in peril on the sea.

2 O Saviour, whose almighty word
  The winds and waves submissive heard,
Who walkedst on the foaming deep,
And calm amid its rage didst sleep:
    O hear us when we cry to thee
    For those in peril on the sea.

3 O sacred Spirit, who didst brood
  Upon the chaos dark and rude,
Who bad'st its angry tumult cease,
And gavest light and life and peace:
    O hear us when we cry to thee
    For those in peril on the sea.

4 O Trinity of love and power,
  Our brethren shield in danger's hour;
From rock and tempest, fire and foe,
Protect them wheresoe'er they go:
    And ever let there rise to thee
    Glad hymns of praise from land and sea.

161   *G. W. Briggs, 1875–1959.*

LORD, in the hollow of thy hand
  Unfathomed lies the boundless deep,
Whose billows rage at thy command,
And at thy bidding sink to sleep.

2 Thy way is on the pathless sea;
  In farthest coasts still thou art near:
And fearing, loving, trusting thee,
No peril shall thy servants fear.

3 When, swept by wind and wave, they breast
  The fury of the winter gale,
On thee their valiant hearts shall rest,
Assured that thou canst never fail.

4 When the black mantle of the night,
  Or shrouding mists, white-robed, by day,
Have veiled the perils from their sight,
Be thou their guide upon their way.

5 Their way is sure, whate'er betide,
  Whose mind on thee, O Lord, is stayed:
In life and death still by thy side,
They journey onward unafraid.

THE SCHOOL

Commemoration

162   *G. W. Briggs, 1875–1959.*

OUR Father, by whose servants
  Our house was built of old,
Whose hand hath crowned her children
    With blessings manifold,
For thine unfailing mercies
    Far-strewn along our way,
With all who passed before us,
    We praise thy name to-day.

2 The changeful years unresting
    Their silent course have sped,
New comrades ever bringing
    In comrades' steps to tread:
And some are long forgotten,
    Long spent their hopes and fears:
Safe rest they in thy keeping,
    Who changest not with years.

3 They reap not where they laboured,
    We reap what they have sown;
Our harvest may be garnered
    By ages yet unknown.
The days of old have dowered us
    With gifts beyond all praise:
Our Father, make us faithful
    To serve the coming days.

4 Before us and beside us,
    Still holden in thine hand,
A cloud unseen of witness,
    Our elder comrades stand:
One family unbroken,
    We join, with one acclaim,
One heart, one voice uplifting,
    To glorify thy name.

Loughborough School Hymn (adapted, by permission).

(NOTE.—*Schools with a known founder may prefer, in verse 1, the original version—'servant'; and ancient foundations may prefer the original of verse 2.*

Four hundred years enduring,
    From age to following age,
A hundred generations
    Have built our heritage:

Their name is long forgotten,
    Long spent their hopes and fears:
Safe rest they in thy keeping,
    Who changest not with years.)

163

H. J. Buckoll, 1803–71.

Assembly

LORD, behold us with thy blessing,
  Once again assembled here;
Onward be our footsteps pressing,
  In thy love and faith and fear:
      Still protect us
  By thy presence ever near.

2 For thy mercy we adore thee,
    For this rest upon our way;
  Lord, again we bow before thee,
    Speed our labours day by day:
        Mind and spirit
    With thy choicest gifts array.

Dismissal

LORD, dismiss us with thy blessing;
  Thanks for mercies past receive;
Pardon all, their faults confessing;
  Time that's lost may all retrieve:
      May thy children
  Ne'er again thy Spirit grieve.

2 Let thy Father-hand be shielding
    All who here shall meet no more;
  May their seed-time past be yielding
    Year by year a richer store:
        Those returning
    Make more faithful than before.

End of Term or School Year

164

J. E. Rankin, 1828–1904.

GOD be with you till we meet again;
  By his counsels guide, uphold you,
  With his sheep securely fold you:
God be with you till we meet again.

2 God be with you till we meet again;
   'Neath his wings protecting hide you,
   Daily manna still provide you:
God be with you till we meet again.

3 God be with you till we meet again;
   When life's perils thick confound you,
   Put his arm unfailing round you:
God be with you till we meet again.

4 God be with you till we meet again;
   Keep love's banner floating o'er you,
   Smite death's threatening wave before you:
God be with you till we meet again.

NATIONAL AND INTERNATIONAL HYMNS

165   *Rudyard Kipling, 1865–1936.*

Land of our birth, we pledge to thee
Our love and toil in the years to be;
When we are grown and take our place,
As men and women with our race.

FATHER in Heaven who lovest all,
O help thy children when they call,
That they may build from age to age
An undefilèd heritage.

2 Teach us to bear the yoke in youth,
With steadfastness and careful truth;
That, in our time thy grace may give
The truth whereby the nations live.

3 Teach us to rule ourselves alway,
Controlled and cleanly night and day;
That we may bring, if need arise,
No maimed or worthless sacrifice.

4 Teach us to look in all our ends
On thee for judge, and not our friends;
That we, with thee, may walk uncowed
By fear or favour of the crowd.

5 Teach us the strength that cannot seek,
   By deed or thought, to hurt the weak;
   That, under thee, we may possess
   Man's strength to comfort man's distress.

6 Teach us delight in simple things,
   And mirth that has no bitter springs;
   Forgiveness free of evil done,
   And love to all men 'neath the sun.

   Land of our birth, our faith, our pride,
   For whose dear sake our fathers died;
   O Motherland, we pledge to thee,
   Head, heart, and hand through the years to be!

(*For National Hymns, in addition to hymns in this section, see*
also 120, 128; *and for International,* 30, 96, 99, 134–8, 140.)

166   *William Blake,* 1757–1827.

AND did those feet in ancient time
   Walk upon England's mountains green?
And was the holy Lamb of God
   On England's pleasant pastures seen?
And did the countenance divine
   Shine forth upon our clouded hills?
And was Jerusalem builded here
   Among those dark satanic mills?

2 Bring me my bow of burning gold!
   Bring me my arrows of desire!
Bring me my spear! O clouds, unfold!
   Bring me my chariot of fire!
I will not cease from mental fight,
   Nor shall my sword sleep in my hand,
Till we have built Jerusalem
   In England's green and pleasant land.

167   *Rudyard Kipling,* 1865–1936.

GOD of our fathers, known of old,
   Lord of our far-flung battle-line,
Beneath whose awful hand we hold
   Dominion over palm and pine—
Lord God of Hosts, be with us yet,
Lest we forget—lest we forget!

2 The tumult and the shouting dies;
        The captains and the kings depart:
Still stands thine ancient sacrifice,
        An humble and a contrite heart.
Lord God of Hosts, be with us yet,
Lest we forget—lest we forget!

3 Far-called, our navies melt away;
        On dune and headland sinks the fire:
Lo, all our pomp of yesterday
        Is one with Nineveh and Tyre!
Judge of the Nations, spare us yet,
Lest we forget—lest we forget!

*4 If, drunk with sight of power, we loose
        Wild tongues that have not thee in awe,
Such boastings as the Gentiles use,
        Or lesser breeds without the Law—
Lord God of Hosts, be with us yet,
Lest we forget—lest we forget!

5 For heathen heart that puts her trust
        In reeking tube and iron shard,
All valiant dust that builds on dust,
        And guarding, calls not thee to guard,
For frantic boast and foolish word—
Thy mercy on thy people, Lord!

168   *Sir Cecil Spring Rice, 1859–1918.*

I VOW to thee, my country—all earthly things
        above—
Entire and whole and perfect, the service of my
        love,
The love that asks no question: the love that stands
        the test,
That lays upon the altar the dearest and the best:
The love that never falters, the love that pays the
        price,
The love that makes undaunted the final sacrifice.

2 And there's another country, I've heard of long
   ago—
   Most dear to them that love her, most great to them
   that know—
   We may not count her armies: we may not see her
   King—
   Her fortress is a faithful heart, her pride is suffer-
   ing—
   And soul by soul and silently her shining bounds
   increase,
   And her ways are ways of gentleness and all her
   paths are peace.

169   *J. Russell Lowell*, 1819–91.

   MEN! whose boast it is that ye
       Come of fathers brave and free,
   If there breathe on earth a slave,
   Are ye truly free and brave?
   If ye do not feel the chain,
   When it works a brother's pain,
   Are ye not base slaves indeed,
   Slaves unworthy to be freed?

2 Is true freedom but to break
   Fetters for our own dear sake,
   And, with leathern hearts, forget
   That we owe mankind a debt?
   No! true freedom is to share
   All the chains our brothers wear,
   And, with heart and hand, to be
   Earnest to make others free!

3 They are slaves who fear to speak
   For the fallen and the weak;
   They are slaves who will not choose
   Hatred, scoffing and abuse,
   Rather than in silence shrink
   From the truth they needs must think;
   They are slaves who dare not be
   In the right with two or three.

170   *Julia Ward Howe*, 1819–1910.

M INE eyes have seen the glory of the coming
       of the Lord:
He is trampling out the vintage where the grapes
    of wrath are stored;
He hath loosed the fateful lightning of his terrible
    swift sword:
  His Truth is marching on.

*2 I have seen him in the watch-fires of a hundred
    circling camps;
They have builded him an altar in the evening
    dews and damps;
I have read his righteous sentence by the dim and
    flaring lamps:
  His Day is marching on.

*3 I have read a fiery gospel, writ in burnished rows
    of steel:
'As ye deal with my contemners, so with you my
    grace shall deal;
Let the Hero born of woman crush the serpent
    with his heel,
  Since God is marching on.'

4 He has sounded forth the trumpet that shall never
    call retreat;
He is sifting out the hearts of men before his judge-
    ment-seat;
O, be swift my soul to answer him; be jubilant,
    my feet!
  Our God is marching on.

5 In the beauty of the lilies Christ was born across
    the sea,
With a glory in his bosom that transfigures you
    and me;
As he died to make men holy, let us die to make
    men free,
  While God is marching on.

6 He is coming like the glory of the morning on the
    wave;
  He is wisdom to the mighty, he is succour to the
    brave;
  So the world shall be his footstool, and the soul of
    time his slave:
      Our God is marching on.

171   *J. S. Arkwright*, 1872–1954.

O VALIANT hearts, who to your glory came
  Through dust of conflict and through battle
    flame;
Tranquil you lie, your knightly virtue proved,
Your memory hallowed in the land you loved.

*2 Proudly you gathered, rank on rank, to war,
As who had heard God's message from afar;
All you had hoped for, all you had, you gave
To save mankind—yourself you scorned to save.

*3 Splendid you passed, the great surrender made,
Into the light that never more shall fade;
Deep your contentment in that blest abode,
Who wait the last clear trumpet-call of God.

4 Long years ago, as earth lay dark and still,
Rose a loud cry upon a lonely hill,
While in the frailty of our human clay,
Christ, our Redeemer, passed the self-same way.

5 Still stands his Cross from that dread hour to this,
Like some bright star above the dark abyss;
Still, through the veil, the Victor's pitying eyes
Look down to bless our lesser Calvaries.

6 These were his servants, in his steps they trod,
Following through death the martyred Son of God:
Victor he rose; victorious too shall rise
They who have drunk his cup of sacrifice.

7 O risen Lord, O shepherd of our dead,
Whose Cross has bought them and whose staff has
    led,
In glorious hope their proud and sorrowing land
Commits her children to thy gracious hand.

NATIONAL ANTHEM

172

GOD save our gracious Queen,
Long live our noble Queen,
God save the Queen!
Send her victorious,
Happy and glorious,
Long to reign over us;
God save the Queen!

The Motherland

2 One realm of races four,
Blest ever more and more,
God save our land!
Home of the brave and free,
Set in the silver sea,
True nurse of chivalry,
God save our land!

The Commonwealth

3 Of many a race and birth,
One Empire, wide as earth,
As ocean wide,
Brothers in war and peace,
Brothers, that war may cease;
God, who hath given increase,
Still guard and guide.

(On general occasions the following version of v. 3 may be preferred.)

Of many a race and birth
From utmost ends of earth,
God save us all!
Bid strife and hatred cease,
Bid hope and joy increase,
Spread universal peace,
God save us all!

GRACE BEFORE MEALS

1

G. W. Briggs, 1875-1959.

OUR Father, for our daily bread
Accept our praise and hear our prayer.
By thee all living souls are fed:
    Thy bounty and thy loving care
    With all thy children let us share.

2

E. Rutter Leatham, 1870-1939.

THANK you for the world so sweet;
    Thank you for the food we eat;
Thank you for the birds that sing:
Thank you, God, for everything.

CAROLS

Christmas and after

1

J. Montgomery, 1771–1854.

ANGELS, from the realms of glory,
Wing your flight o'er all the earth;
Ye who sang creation's story
Now proclaim Messiah's birth:
Come and worship
Christ, the new-born King.
Come and worship,
Worship Christ, the new-born King.

2 Shepherds in the fields abiding,
Watching o'er your flocks by night,
God with man is now residing,
Yonder shines the infant Light:

3 Sages, leave your contemplations;
Brighter visions beam afar;
Seek the great Desire of Nations;
Ye have seen his natal star:

*4 Saints before the altar bending,
Watching long in hope and fear,
Suddenly the Lord, descending,
In his temple shall appear:

5 Though an infant now we view him,
He shall fill his Father's throne,
Gather all the nations to him;
Every knee shall then bow down:
Come and worship
Christ, the new-born King.
Come and worship,
Worship Christ, the new-born King.

2

German, 16th century. Tr. P. Dearmer.

A BOY was born in Bethlehem,
In Bethlehem;
Rejoice for that, Jerusalem!
Alleluya, Alleluya.

2 For low he lay within a stall,
          Within a stall,
   Who rules for ever over all:

3 He let himself a servant be,
          A servant be,
   That all mankind he might set free:

4 Then praise the Word of God who came,
          Of God who came,
   To dwell within a human frame:

5 And praised be God in threefold might,
          And glory bright,
   Eternal, good, and infinite!

3   *P. Dearmer, 1867–1936, from the Czech.*

FROM out of a wood did a cuckoo fly
          Cuckoo,
He came to a manger with joyful cry,
          Cuckoo;
He hopped, he curtsied, round he flew,
And loud his jubilation grew,
          Cuckoo, cuckoo, cuckoo.

2 A pigeon flew over to Galilee,
          Vrercroo,
   He strutted, and cooed, and was full of glee,
          Vrercroo,
   And showed with jewelled wings unfurled,
   His joy that Christ was in the world,
          Vrercroo, vrercroo, vrercroo.

3 A dove settled down upon Nazareth,
          Tsucroo,
   And tenderly chanted with all his breath,
          Tsucroo:
   'O you,' he cooed, 'so good and true,
   My beauty do I give to you—
          Tsucroo, tsucroo, tsucroo.'

Christmas: New Year

4

GOD rest you merry, gentlemen,
   Let nothing you dismay,
Remember Christ our Saviour
   Was born on Christmas Day,
To save poor souls from Satan's power
   Which had long time gone astray,
And it's tidings of comfort and joy, comfort and
      joy:
   And it's tidings of comfort and joy.

2 From God that is our Father
      The blessèd angels came,
   Unto some certain shepherds,
      With tidings of the same;
   That there was born in Bethlehem,
      The Son of God by name.
   And it's tidings of comfort and joy.

3 Go, fear not, said God's angels,
      Let nothing you affright,
   For there is born in Bethlehem,
      Of a pure Virgin bright,
   One able to advance you,
      And throw down Satan quite.
   And it's tidings of comfort and joy.

4 The shepherds at those tidings
      Rejoicèd much in mind,
   And left their flocks a feeding
      In tempest storms of wind,
   And straight they came to Bethlehem,
      The Son of God to find.
   And it's tidings of comfort and joy.

5 Now when they came to Bethlehem,
      Where our sweet Saviour lay,
   They found him in a manger,
      Where oxen feed on hay,
   The blessèd Virgin kneeling down,
      Unto the Lord did pray.
   And it's tidings of comfort and joy.

6 With sudden joy and gladness
   The shepherds were beguiled,
To see the Babe of Israel
   Before his mother mild,
On them with joy and cheerfulness
   Rejoice each mother's child.
And it's tidings of comfort and joy.

(Before Christmas only.)

7 Now to the Lord sing praises,
   All you within this place,
Like we true loving brethren,
   Each other to embrace,
For the merry time of Christmas
   Is drawing on apace.
And it's tidings of comfort and joy.

(*'God rest you merry'* means *'God keep you merry'*.)

5   *Isaac Watts, 1674–1748.*

HUSH! my dear, lie still and slumber;
   Holy angels guard thy bed!
Heavenly blessings without number
   Gently falling on thy head.

2 How much better thou'rt attended
   Than the Son of God could be
When from heaven he descended,
   And became a child like thee.

3 Soft and easy is thy cradle;
   Coarse and hard thy Saviour lay,
When his birthplace was a stable
   And his softest bed was hay.

4 May'st thou live to know and fear him,
   Trust and love him all thy days:
Then go dwell for ever near him,
   See his face and sing his praise.

Christmas: Epiphany

6 *From an old Dorset Church-gallery book.*

REJOICE and be merry in songs and in mirth!
O praise our Redeemer, all mortals on earth!
For this is the birthday of Jesus our King,
Who brought us salvation—his praises we'll sing!

2 A heavenly vision appeared in the sky;
Vast numbers of angels the Shepherds did spy,
Proclaiming the birthday of Jesus our King,
Who brought us salvation—his praises we'll sing!

3 Likewise a bright star in the sky did appear,
Which led the Wise Men from the east to draw
near;
They found the Messiah, sweet Jesus our King,
Who brought us salvation—his praises we'll sing!

4 And when they were come, they their treasures
unfold,
And unto him offered myrrh, incense, and gold.
So blessèd for ever be Jesus our King,
Who brought us salvation—his praises we'll sing!

Epiphany

7 *J. H. Hopkins, Jun., 1820–91.*

The Kings.

WE three kings of Orient are;
Bearing gifts we traverse afar
Field and fountain, moor and mountain,
Following yonder star:
O star of wonder, star of night,
Star with royal beauty bright,
Westward leading, still proceeding,
Guide us to thy perfect light.

Melchior.

2 Born a king on Bethlehem plain,
Gold I bring, to crown him again—
King for ever, ceasing never,
Over us all to reign:

Gaspar.

3 Frankincense to offer have I;
Incense owns a Deity nigh:
Prayer and praising, all men raising,
Worship him, God most high:

Balthazar.

4 Myrrh is mine; its bitter perfume
Breathes a life of gathering gloom;
Sorrowing, sighing, bleeding, dying,
Sealed in the stone-cold tomb:

All.

5 Glorious now, behold him arise,
King, and God, and sacrifice!
Heaven sings alleluya,
Alleluya the earth replies:

Note.—The tradition identifying the 'wise men' with
three Kings is very ancient; though, needless to say, there
is no historical foundation for it. Such pleasant fancies,
though they would be out of place in hymns, are fully
understood in carols.

This carol lends itself to dramatic rendering. In some
schools, at carol services, the three 'Kings' enter in pro-
cession, bearing symbolic gifts.

All the verses have the same melody; but in verse 5 the
metre slightly varies.

Nativity: Passiontide to Eastertide

8 *Sans Day.* *Cornish.*

NOW the holly bears a berry as white as the milk,
And Mary bore Jesus, who was wrapt up in silk:
*And Mary bore Jesus Christ our Saviour for to be,
And the first tree in the green-wood, it was the
holly, holly, holly!
And the first tree in the green-wood, it was the
holly.*

2 Now the holly bears a berry as green as the grass,
  And Mary bore Jesus, who died on the cross:

3 Now the holly bears a berry as black as the coal,
  And Mary bore Jesus, who died for us all:

4 Now the holly bears a berry, as blood is it red,
  Then trust we our Saviour, who rose from the dead:

The Sans Day or St. Day Carol has been so named
because the melody and the first three verses were taken
down at St. Day in the parish of Gwennap, Cornwall.
St. Day or St. They was a Breton saint whose cult was
widely spread in Armorican Cornwall. We owe the carol
to the kindness of the Rev. G. H. Doble, to whom
Mr. W. D. Watson sang it after hearing an old man,
Mr. Thomas Beard, sing it at St. Day. A version in
Cornish was subsequently published ('Ma gron war'n
gelinen') with a fourth stanza, here translated and added
to Mr. Beard's English version.

Christmas and General

9   *Cölner Psalter, 1638. Pr. P. Dearmer.*

TO us in Bethlehem city
  Was born a little son;
In him all gentle graces
  Were gathered into one,
      Eia, Eia,
  Were gathered into one.

2 And all our love and fortune
    Lie in his mighty hands;
  Our sorrows, joys, and failures,
    He sees and understands,
        Eia, Eia,
    He sees and understands.

3 O Shepherd ever near us,
    We'll go where thou dost lead;
  No matter where the pasture,
    With thee at hand to feed,
        Eia, Eia,
    With thee at hand to feed.

4 No grief shall part us from thee,
   However sharp the edge:
      We'll serve, and do thy bidding—
      O take our hearts in pledge!
         Eia, Eia,
         Take thou our hearts in pledge!

(*Eia is a Latin exclamation of joy, and is pronounced 'iyah'.*)

Spring

10   *Jan Struther, 1901–53.*

ROUND the earth a message runs:
   Awake, awake, you drowsy ones!
Now leaps the sap in every stem
To chant the winter's requiem.
   No more of sloth and dullness sing:
   Sing love, sing joy, for Christ is King!

2 Round the earth a message runs:
   Arise, arise, you doleful ones!
Cast off your chains, you captives all
Who long have lain in sorrow's thrall.
   No more of grief and anguish sing:
   Sing love, sing joy, for Christ is King!

3 Round the earth a message runs:
   For shame, for shame, you brawling ones!
You shall more true adventure find
In friendliness of heart and mind.
   No more of hate and envy sing:
   Sing love, sing joy, for Christ is King!

4 Round the earth a message runs:
   Rejoice, rejoice, you happy ones!
Now fall the gods of wrath and pain,
Now comes your Prince of Joy to reign;
   To him your brave allegiance sing:
   Sing love, sing joy, for Christ is King!

A MODERN BENEDICITE

J. S. Blackie, 1809–95.

ANGELS holy,
 High and lowly,
  Sing the praises of the Lord!
Earth and sky, all living nature,
Man, the stamp of thy Creator,
  Praise ye, praise ye God the Lord!
   Sun and moon bright
   Night and noon light,
  Starry temples azure-floored,
Cloud and rain, and wild wind's madness,
Sons of God that shout for gladness,
  Praise ye, praise ye God the Lord!

2   Ocean hoary,
      Tell his glory,
  Cliffs, where tumbling seas have roared,
Pulse of waters, blithely beating,
Wave advancing, wave retreating,
  Praise ye, praise ye God the Lord!
   Rolling river,
   Praise him ever,
  From the mountain's deep vein poured;
Silver fountain, clearly gushing,
Troubled torrent, madly rushing,
  Praise ye, praise ye God the Lord.

3   Rock and highland,
      Wood and island,
  Crag, where eagle's pride hath soared,
Mighty mountains, purple-breasted,
Peaks cloud-cleaving, snowy-crested,
  Praise ye, praise ye God the Lord!
   Birds, whose pinion
   Gives dominion
  In sky-regions deep and broad,
Flocks that stray o'er hills unbounded,
Herds with verdant plains surrounded,
  Praise ye, praise ye God the Lord!

4   Bond and free man,
    Land and sea man,
  Earth with peoples widely stored,
 Wanderer lone o'er prairies ample,
 Full-voiced choir in costly temple,
  Praise ye, praise ye God the Lord!
    Praise him ever,
    Bounteous Giver!
  Praise him, Father, Friend, and Lord!
 Each glad soul its free course winging,
 Each glad voice its free song singing,
  Praise the great and mighty Lord!

(*Note.*—The words in italics may be sung by a semi-
choir, in two parts.)

INDEX OF FIRST LINES

CAROLS

PRINTED IN GREAT BRITAIN BY
RICHARD CLAY
(THE CHAUCER PRESS), LTD.
BUNGAY, SUFFOLK